Critical Guides to Spanish Texts

EDITED BY J.E. VAREY AND A.D. DEYERMOND

Peter Standish

Senior Lecturer in Spanish
University of Stirling

Grant & Cutler Ltd *in association with*
Tamesis Books Ltd 1982

© Grant & Cutler Ltd
1982
ISBN 0 7293 0135 4

I.S.B.N. 84-499-6350-8

DEPÓSITO LEGAL: V. 1.846-1983

Printed in Spain by
Artes Gráficas Soler, S.A., Valencia
for
GRANT & CUTLER LTD
11 BUCKINGHAM STREET, LONDON, W.C.2

The text of the novel is that of the first edition, published by Seix Barral, Barcelona, 1962, and reprinted many times thereafter.

References to the works listed in the Bibliographical Note give the number of the work in italics, followed by page numbers.

Shortly after _____
ciudad y los perros were ___
symbolic act. The act took place on the p__
Leoncio Prado Academy, for the school which provided
setting for Vargas Llosa's first major, explosive novel exists in
real life.[1] Indeed, all his novels are firmly rooted in his own real
experiences, a fact which goes some way towards justifying
Gerald Martin's provocative assertion (5, p.117) that: 'Vargas
Llosa no ha inventado nunca nada.'

Not surprisingly, what was designed as an act of punishment
by fire served instead to kindle the author's reputation and sell
more copies of the offending book. The military governors of
the Leoncio Prado school had argued that Vargas Llosa was a
man of sick mind and an enemy of his native Peru. Further, they
attempted to discredit him by making public certain details from
the time he spent in that school: they revealed that he had a poor
academic record and had been subjected to a considerable
number of 'arrests' for bad conduct. It is unlikely that these
revelations did much to harm the author's public standing. As
for the governors' belief that this amounted to proof that Vargas
Llosa lacked the qualities of a good writer, it can only be
regarded as exceedingly naïve.

The Leoncio Prado was Vargas Llosa's fourth school. He was
born in 1936 in Arequipa, the principal city of southern Peru.
Since his parents had separated shortly before his birth, he
began life with his mother in her parents' house. When he was
barely a year old he was moved to Cochabamba, Bolivia, where
his grandfather had been posted as consul. Vargas Llosa's life
and early schooling in Bolivia were happy and cosseted until the

[1] Leoncio Prado was a military hero in the War of the Pacific (1879-83).

family returned to Peru in 1945, this time to Piura in the north. (Piura was to be a setting for his second major work, *La casa verde*.) There he spent an unhappy year in a school where his classmates were rather older than he was. The reconciliation of Vargas Llosa's parents brought him back to Lima. The Leoncio Prado Academy, which he entered in 1950, was unlike the Catholic day-schools he had so far experienced; it served as a kind of corrective institution for problem children of various origins. In this spirit, Vargas Llosa's father saw the school as a means of making a man of his son and dispelling his fanciful literary proclivities.

According to Oviedo (*6*, p. 20), even today Vargas Llosa experiences periods of depression on Sunday afternoons, the time when, years ago, he would gather together his possessions, after a week-end at home, to return to the military school. This was evidently a period when he was unhappy and maladjusted, one which made a profound impression on him. Yet, just as evidently, it was the time when literature began to engage his serious interest: not only did he read a great deal, he also started to write a little, to the satisfaction of his doting grandparents and to the alarm of his father. If his father and the school conspired to turn writing into an outlawed activity, it was only natural that this activity should gain in attraction for the boy:

Esa vocación se afirmó y creció un poco secretamente. Entonces, mi rebelión contra el Leoncio Prado se volcó un poco hacia la literatura. Ya en esa época la literatura se convirtió en una cosa muy importante para mí. También era clandestina. Porque en el colegio había que evitarla. (*4*, p. 434)

He lasted two years in the military college, returning to Piura for his final school year. Soon he was at work as a journalist and also wrote his first play, *La huida del Inca*, which was staged in 1952. The play was no great success; neither was the poetry he tried at about that time. After that, as a student of literature and law in Lima, he struggled to subsist with the aid of several part-time jobs, mostly relying on his pen. Still a student, he made his first marriage, later to inform his humorous novel of 1977, *La*

... . Eventually his various journalistic
....

los perros. ...
Llosa was now entering a long period of ......
native country and from the continent at large. Briefly, and on
several occasions, he has returned to both since the late fifties,
but for a long time he settled in neither.

The return fare to Lima had been used instead to move from
Madrid to Paris. For weeks he was without work before
beginning a succession of posts in language teaching,
journalism, broadcasting. In this last capacity, working for
Radio-Télévision Française, Vargas Llosa found security and
the time to write in the evenings, avoiding the sterile round of
cafés and conversation in which other artists tended to be
involved. Like Julio Cortázar, the exiled Argentinian writer who
was also established in Paris and whom he saw as something of a
model, Vargas Llosa led an austere and disciplined existence. He
set about filling the gaps in his literary education; he revised and
pruned his manuscript, then under the title of *Los impostores*.
The discussion the author had with Elena Poniatowska (7)
shows how life in Peru did not favour the activities of a creative
writer and explains why he personally found it easier to work in
Paris or London. To begin with, writers in Peru live apart from
society, being thought of as, at best, eccentric. There is a high
level of illiteracy in the country and, according to Vargas Llosa,
even middle-class Peruvians are illiterate in a sense, if one
compares them with their counterparts in Chile or Argentina. In
these last two countries a literature of sorts has always been

---

[2]Many critics indicate that he was awarded the degree for a thesis on Rubén
Darío, but it was in fact years later, and for his book *García Márquez: historia
de un deicidio*, that he gained his doctorate.

fostered; not so in Peru. On the other hand, while working for French radio or teaching in England (at Queen Mary and King's Colleges in the University of London) Vargas Llosa could buy books, eat as well as any other skilled worker, and find six to eight hours a day to satisfy his passion for writing.

In 1959 Vargas Llosa had won Spain's Leopoldo Alas prize for a collection of stories called *Los jefes*, published in Barcelona. Only Buenos Aires and Mexico City can rival Spain's two main cities in the field of publishing in Spanish. Yet Spain's literary prizes are too numerous to be always significant: *Los jefes* attracted little attention and certainly gave no guarantee of the success, or even publication, of *La ciudad y los perros*. It was a chance meeting with the publisher Carlos Barral that encouraged Vargas Llosa to submit his manuscript for the fifth annual Biblioteca Breve contest. The title had by now become *La morada del héroe*. For the first time in the history of the contest the verdict of the jury was unanimous and for the first time, too, the prize did not go to a Spaniard. In 1962 *La ciudad y los perros* was published with its definitive title.

The Premio Biblioteca Breve was to be the first of several major awards and Vargas Llosa, not yet thirty, moved smartly to the crest of the wave of new Latin-American fiction which was exciting the world's attention. (To mention only two other major works of that time, Carlos Fuentes' *La muerte de Artemio Cruz* appeared in that same year and Julio Cortázar's *Rayuela* only months afterwards.) Reprints of *La ciudad y los perros* rapidly followed; there were editions in Lima and Buenos Aires, and numerous translations.

THE WRITER AS REBEL

La casa verde, Vargas Llosa's second major work, was to confirm his reputation and bring more honours. He won three prizes, most especially a new one named after the Venezuelan novelist, and sometime president, Rómulo Gallegos. The money value of the Gallegos prize was at that time equivalent to some £10,000 and therefore second in value only to the Nobel award for literature. At a ceremony in Caracas the ageing Gallegos

⋯⋯ Vargas Llosa, who responded with
⋯⋯ ⋯⋯ as had his

attempt to suppr⋯
alternatively it could tolerate literature ⋯
subversion of the *status quo*.

Typically, Vargas Llosa had begun by confusing his audience.
He opened by recalling the fate of one Oquendo de Amat, a
much-ignored poet who had lived in poverty in Lima, made his
way, despite torture and imprisonment, to Europe, died in the
mountains of Castile, and even had his grave obliterated by the
guns of the Civil War. Here was a case of extreme misfortune to
contrast with the good fortune that had befallen Vargas Llosa
himself; the truth was that most Latin-American writers had a
poor time of it, working in countries which gave no
encouragement, which lacked the means of publication and
whose people scarcely read. Societies like these were not only
havens of ignorance, they were riddled with injustice, with social
inequalities, poverty and corruption. The writer was therefore a
rebel with a cause, or rather with a double cause, one cultural
and one social.

That Vargas Llosa should have gone on, as he did, to cite
Cuba as an example of social justice brought about by changes
which he thought inevitable in all Latin America, was bound to
provoke a furore. The writer performed a useful role, he argued,
whether he was lauded or persecuted, only insofar as he made
his fellow men face 'el espectáculo no siempre grato de sus
miserias y tormentas'.

Sólo si cumple esta condición es útil la literatura a la
sociedad. Ella contribuye al perfeccionamiento humano

[3]'La literatura es fuego' was first printed in *Mundo Nuevo* (Paris), 17 (1967),
and is reprinted, for example, in *9*.

impidiendo el marasmo espiritual, la autosatisfacción, el inmovilismo, la parálisis humana, el reblandecimiento intelectual o moral. Su misión es agitar, inquietar, alarmar, mantener a los hombres en una constante insatisfacción de sí mismos: su función es estimular sin tregua la voluntad de cambio y de mejora, aun cuando para ello deba emplear las armas más hirientas y nocivas. Es preciso que todos lo comprendan de una vez: mientras más duros y terribles sean los escritos de un autor contra su país, más intensa será la pasión que lo una a él. Porque en el dominio de la literatura la violencia es una prueba de amor. (*8*, p. 20)

In the course of this study I shall attempt an assessment of Vargas Llosa as a social commentator and discuss whether he writes a sophisticated kind of propaganda. For the moment, two other events in his past should be mentioned, since they serve to counter any temptation to compartmentalise Vargas Llosa as simply another writer motivated (and limited) by a particular ideological standpoint. At about the time of the Caracas speech he began championing the causes of writers oppressed by communist régimes. Of Sinyavsky and Daniel in the Soviet Union he had written a defence published in the first issue of *Mundo Nuevo*,[4] later elaborating as follows:

Aun en el momento del triunfo del socialismo el escritor debe seguir siendo un descontento... Censurar a los que condenaron a Siniavski y Daniel no es hacer la menor concesión al capitalismo o al imperialismo. Hay que defender la libertad de creación. (*9*, p. 63)

In Cuba itself there arose the case of the poet Heberto Padilla: suffice it to say that in 1971 Vargas Llosa broke with the Cuban revolutionary régime. A Marxist he indeed was (see *4*, p. 426), but he would oppose both injustice and dogmatism in any context.

The image of the writer as a perpetual malcontent is one which the author has never relinquished, although in an article published in Cuba in 1966 he makes what I believe is a crucial proviso: he allows that an artist is first and foremost just that,

[4] 'Una insurrección permanente', *Mundo Nuevo* (Paris), 1 (1966), 94-5.

an artist:

...............................concepción política y al

him.

In the USA, in Western Europe, to be a writer means, generally, first (and usually only) to assume a personal responsibility. That is, a responsibility to achieve in the most rigorous and authentic way a work which, for its artistic values and originality, enriches the language and culture of one's country. In Peru, in Bolivia, in Nicaragua etcetera, on the contrary, to be a writer means, at the same time, to assume a social responsibility: at the same time that you develop a personal literary work, you should serve, through your writing but also through your actions, as an active participant in the solution of the economic, political and cultural problems of your society. (*11*, p. 6)

Depending on one's own political views, either Vargas Llosa has become educated to the realities of life in the countries he refers to early in the preceding paragraph, or else success has seduced him into complicity with their systems, made him oblivious of their faults. Given his thoroughness and persistence in his work, the latter seems to me an unlikely alternative: it is surely the case that the iniquities of life in Latin America are the more pressingly obvious, and that they are the ones which form part of Vargas Llosa's personal inheritance.

VARGAS LLOSA'S THEORY OF THE NOVEL

His many published interviews, articles and lectures, together with two major works of criticism (*12* and *13*) have provided us with a full picture of Vargas Llosa's theory of literature. He regards the novel as the prime genre and one which subsumes

other genres—'género invasor'—making use of them for its own
purposes. According to Vargas Llosa the origin of the modern
novel can be pinpointed quite precisely in the medieval romances
of chivalry; he makes two claims to support this view. The
romances of chivalry were disinterested, had no ulterior moral
or exemplary purpose, in contrast to the didacticism that was
prevalent in previous literature. Indeed, these romances were
subversive of the established order and therefore censured by it;
it was claimed they diverted man's attention from God.
Secondly, chivalresque romances sought to represent life in all
its complexity and from many standpoints, a kind of literary
enterprise for which Vargas Llosa was to use the term
'totalizing':

> Lo que más sorprende al lector en las novelas de caballería,
> es la habilidad del narrador para capturar la realidad a
> todos sus niveles. Ahí vemos transcurrir la vida cotidiana
> de la Edad Media...estas novelas escritas en un lenguaje a
> veces bárbaro, son como tentativas de abarcar la realidad a
> todos sus niveles, pretenden decirlo todo, quieren
> abarcarlo todo. Yo creo que las mejores novelas son las
> que se han acercado a esta posición, es decir, las que
> expresan las cosas desde todos los puntos de vista...
> Considero que las novelas que dan sólo una dimensión de
> la realidad, las novelas de tipo psicológico, exclusivamente
> psicológico, tienden a mutilar la realidad; las grandes
> novelas no mutilan la realidad, sino que la ensanchan; no
> sólo son novedosas, sino que dan un testimonio nuevo, son
> totalizadoras. (*14*, p. 79)

Vargas Llosa has returned to these words, or others very close
to them, on many occasions since, always insisting on the same
vital characteristics. One work to which he constantly refers in
this connexion is *Tirant lo blanc* by the Valencian Joanot
Martorell (see *15*); although few would go so far, Vargas Llosa
rates Martorell's romance above Cervantes' *Don Quixote*.

> En esa novela [*Tirant*] está presentada en cierta forma toda
> la realidad de su tiempo...tanto la dimensión puramente
> mística, espiritual y subjetiva, como una dimensión

Esta tentativa de mostrar la

p. 19)

Over the course of history, he argues, the novel has possible for men to take stock of their situation, of their greatness, their weaknesses and their limits. At times of complacent self-satisfaction, whether individual or national, great novels have not been written; rather it is at times of crisis or decay in the established order that the best writing has been produced. Hence the great period of the Russian novel in the last century, the rise of Proust, Kafka, Joyce at the beginning of this one, and the current 'boom' in Latin America. Yet no great novels arose in times of great national purpose and unity, like the French and Russian revolutions or the North and South American movements for independence (*6*, p. 70).

Vargas Llosa would not agree with those who regard the novel as moribund, if not dead. Although it may be in the doldrums in Europe and the United States, sometimes becoming ever more embroiled in arcane matters of technique, he points out that it is thriving in a Latin America which provides ample cause for the writer's inherent rebelliousness:

> El momento más propicio para la ficción es aquél en el que la realidad deja de tener un sentido preciso para una comunidad histórica... La novelística de las sociedades estables, las ficciones que inspira una realidad histórica no amenazada por un cambio radical inminente—es decir, aquella realidad sostenida aún por la fe del cuerpo social—suelen estar marcadas por el sello de la ironía, del juego formal, del intelectualismo artificioso o el nihilismo cínico. (*17*, pp. 122-3)

Just as the best novels respond to a society in crisis, so too

Vargas Llosa sees them as the result of a kind of personal
tension. The writer is at odds with his environment, feels driven
to portray it by verbal means. He is, in a sense, chosen by his
subject matter (*19*, p. 47). His personal history and situation
have left him with certain obsessions ('demonios personales')
which he must exorcise, on which he must strive to impose some
intellectual discipline through art. The obsessions determine his
themes and over these he has little rational control; yet in the
matter of form, language and style, the intellect takes over (*18*,
p. 82; *13*, p. 87). The inspiration for these particular ideas,
according to Oviedo (*6*, pp. 59, 64), comes from the writings of
Jean-Paul Sartre. To write novels is to represent, by verbal
means, events or situations which derive from the real world the
author knows. All novels are therefore autobiographical in a
very full sense and no analysis of a novel can claim to be
adequate if it fails to take into account the biography of the
author (*19*, p. 33). Vargas Llosa takes issue with those critics, led
by the recently-deceased Roland Barthes, who attempt purely
formal explanations of literary works: to do so, he says, is to
reduce literature to something schematic. Although a verbal
code is, in the end, the sole means by which the writer may try to
represent reality, to investigate that code alone is by definition to
make a partial investigation of the literary work:

> El ecumenismo característico de este género, su voluntad
> totalizadora, de algún modo debe reflejarse en la
> crítica...La crítica capaz de dar cuenta de esa universalidad
> debe ser ella misma universal. (*19*, pp. 19, 20)

A literary work can be assessed internally by relating its form
and technique to its persuasiveness, to the degree to which it is
convincing; it can be assessed externally by relating the fictional
world it portrays to the one it seeks to represent and criticise.
Not that a novel is merely a verbal picture of reality akin to a
photograph; what makes a novel literature rather than simply
social documentation is the 'elemento añadido', that part of
himself which the author contributes, in criticism of or
sympathy with the world he is (re)creating. Despite the very
personal process that is involved in the writing itself, Vargas

... for the novelist to create a work which is

masterpiece *Madame Bovary* appeals to Vargas Llosa
displays characteristics he has always admired: symmetry, rigorous organisation, a sense of progression from a beginning to an end, conclusiveness, self-sufficiency. Vargas Llosa has less sympathy for the open-ended and formally inconclusive type of novel which some of his contemporaries prefer.

Flaubert's novel, moreover, is a total one representing all aspects of reality, encompassing the erotic (hence the title of Vargas Llosa's study of Flaubert, *12*), the psychological, the social and so forth. To achieve this detailed examination of life Flaubert has to play God ('suplantador de Dios'), omnipresent but nowhere apparent. As David Sobrevilla puts it (*20*, p. 31), it is a matter of 'estatuir la ficción como realidad autosuficiente y desaparecer él mismo sin dejar huellas'. In other words, and however paradoxically, the achievement of a detailed, total picture requires that the author's presence is forgotten. Flaubert himself (in a letter to Mlle de Chantepie on 18 March 1887) wrote that:

> L'artiste doit être dans son oeuvre comme Dieu dans la Création, invisible et toutpuissant, qu'on le sente partout mais qu'on ne le voie pas.[5]

Of his own writing Vargas Llosa says:

> trato de que aparezcan esos mundos justificados por sí mismos, como independientes de todo elemento ajeno, de todo ser extraño, como lo sería el autor. (*21*, p.2)

[5]'The artist should be present in his work just as God is in His Creation, almighty and invisible; we should sense his presence everywhere but see him nowhere.' See Flaubert, *Oeuvres complètes* (Paris: Conard, 1902), Vol. IV, p.113.

Once again, here is a respect in which Vargas Llosa parts company with many modern novelists, who are rather inclined self-consciously to remind the reader of the fact that the novelist is at work all the time, that the book being read is an artificial contrivance.

But for Vargas Llosa the illusion of involvement is essential: the reader must feel immersed, caught up in the flow of events:

> Los novelistas que yo admiro y que releo no son nunca los que me exigen ser admirador a la distancia. Son los que arrastran, me arrebatan y me instalan en 'su' mundo nuevo. (*4*, p.439).

Therefore, whatever techniques are used must be sufficiently unobtrusive as to keep the reader close to the action, 'anular la distancia entre el lector y lo narrado' (*14*, p.78); they must prevent the reader from stepping back to make detached judgements during the reading, make him live the action as if in real life. Life, we must remember, is not altogether orderly; thus, despite the organisational discipline involved in creating the fictional world, the impression deliberately given in Vargas Llosa's novels may be one of disorder. All the above considerations lead to a delicate interplay of authorial devices and illusion; the great risk is that the disorder will create too much confusion, the techniques become too apparent and the illusion be undermined.

There are many affinities of purpose, style and content between Vargas Llosa and his French mentor (see *22*). They share the 'condición de galeote', the dedication and exclusive commitment to writing, the refusal to submit to outside pressures, the ideals of objectivity and impartiality, of the self-sufficient narrative with the elimination of the narrator. Flaubert is known to have minutely revised his manuscripts; Vargas Llosa regularly produces a provisional version (which he calls the 'magma'), as much as five times as long as the finished article, before undertaking meticulous and painstaking revisions see *4*, p.428).

To Martorell, Vargas Llosa attributes an early notion of fictional autonomy as well as certain techniques which herald

... f the modern novel. An important example is that of the

imaginative elements:

> ...la realidad reúne, generosamente, lo real objetivo y lo
> real imaginario en una indivisible totalidad en la que
> conviven, sin discriminación de fronteras, hombres de
> carne y hueso y seres de la fantasía y del sueño, personajes
> históricos y criaturas del mito, la razón y la sinrazón, lo
> posible y lo imposible. (*12*, p.177)

Clearly, then, the resulting concept of realism has little to do
with any pretensions to a faithful reflection of the real
world—if, as Malva Filer points out (*22*, p. 504), such a goal
were ever feasible. The author has himself said that all true
novelists are realists; for him the only meaningful distinction is
between lifelike and lifeless writing ('realista' and 'irreal'
respectively). By this yardstick he judges Borges 'realista' and
Corín Tellado 'irreal' (*19*, p.60).

García Márquez may rise to Vargas Llosa's ideal of the total
novel, but it is acknowledged that many modern novelists do not
share that ideal:

> Las tentativas modernas de la novela quieren dar una
> visión de un solo canal, de un solo nivel de realidad. Yo
> estoy, al contrario, por la novela totalizadora, que
> ambiciona abrazar una realidad en todas sus
> fases...mientras más fases consiga dar, la visión de la
> realidad será más amplia y la novela será más completa. (*4*,
> p.440)

Vargas Llosa's independence of mind—Coleman calls it
'critical dissidence' (*25*, p. 24)—is characteristic of the man in
general. Frequently, and with relish, he returns to insisting on

views which are at least unfashionable, at worst simply
outdated. Despite his Marxist sympathies and his Sartrian
notion of writing as an 'insurrección permanente' he has
doggedly (and laudably) refused to try to make propaganda in
his books: 'No escribo para demostrar nada...' (*6*, p. 79). As he
said of the romances of chivalry, the genre is characterized by
disinterestedness; it cannot serve to teach lessons or moralise
(*16*, p. 14). Nor does his apocalyptic view of the novel as the
product of societies in crisis accord at all easily with the widely-
held idea that the genre is bourgeois. Critically, too, as I have
suggested, he is far removed from most major schools of our
day; the critical stance he adopts instead is essentially a
traditional one. According to Gerald Martin:

> El único que se digna renovar y desarrollar lo que ya se
> llama, despectivamente, el realismo burgués, es Vargas
> Llosa, y de ahí irónicamente, su notable originalidad. (*5*,
> p.113)

Whether Martin is also correct in saying that Vargas Llosa
fails to live up to his own precepts, whether there is anything to
Coleman's 'instructive paradox' in the fact that Vargas Llosa is
uncomfortable with the fantastic (*25*, p. 28), are questions we
shall return to in the conclusion. For the moment, it seems
appropriate to give the author the last words, which should now
be fully comprehensible:

> ...representación verbal desinteresada de la realidad
> humana que expresa el mundo en la medida que lo niega,
> que rehace deshaciendo, este deicidio sutil que entendemos
> por novela y que es perpetrado por un hombre que hace las
> veces de suplantador de Dios, nació en Occidente, en la
> alta Edad Media, cuando moría la fe y la razón humana
> iba a reemplazar a Dios como instrumento de comprensión
> de la vida y como principio rector para el gobierno de la
> sociedad. (*17*, p. 121)

chapters. Here, ~
structure of the novel and its use of language.

Commenting on the wide sale of the book in Spain, Andrés Amorós recorded his surprise that this should be the case because it is a difficult novel to read.[6] For many readers, no doubt, the near-pornographic episodes and the relentless sense of action have compensated for any formal complications; yet the fact remains that the author uses his material in a way that forces his reader to accept frequent changes of scene, disturbances of the narrative sequence, shifts of perspective and style. There is absolutely nothing new in an author making demands of this kind on his reader. One has only to glance at the work of the French *nouveaux romanciers* or think of Cortázar's ideal of the *lector cómplice* to conclude that the phenomenon has become commonplace in modern literature, while evidence of it in much earlier writers is not hard to find. Moreover, while *La ciudad y los perros* does undoubtedly make the reader do his share of the work, we shall, I think, discover that Vargas Llosa is in some technical respects a very conservative writer.

To begin the analysis we may note that the elaborate structure of the novel masks a story which is itself quite simple and in essence rather trite. The Leoncio Prado Academy is a boys' school run by soldiers. In it the pupils are drawing lots to see who is to steal the questions for the approaching chemistry exam; the lot falls to Cava, a boy from the mountains. A window is broken during the robbery and when this is discovered the cadets are confined to barracks indefinitely. In his

[6] *Introducción a la novela hispanoamericana actual* (Madrid: Anaya, 1971), p. 166.

desperation to see his girlfriend at the weekend, one of the cadets, a puny misfit nicknamed Esclavo, secretly reveals the robber's identity to the authorities and Cava is expelled from the school. The circle of boys, led by the aggressive Jaguar, suspect that someone has betrayed them. Then, during some military manoeuvres, Esclavo is shot in the head and dies. Suspicion falls on Jaguar, but the authorities, in their anxiety to preserve appearances, promulgate an official statement that there has been an accident. Esclavo's only friend in the school has been Alberto, an intelligent middle-class boy who is fully capable of guarding his own interests; Alberto is now led to break with the other cadets and denounce Jaguar as culprit to one of the officers. However, the authorities prefer the safety of their official version and refuse to reopen the case. Knowing that Alberto has been writing dirty stories to sell to his peers, the school authorities blackmail him into silence. Gamboa, the officer who received the denunciation, the only one who has the boys' respect, and a man of some integrity, finds his career prospects ruined, his faith in the system undermined; although still dutiful, he is transferred to a provincial post where his voice cannot be heard.

This is the story which runs through the period of the boys' academy life; that period is extended backwards, by passages which evoke the life of some of the main characters in pre-college days, and forwards, in the epilogue, to show their reintegration into society.

No violence is done to the chronology of the action as summarized above. However, this fact is not immediately apparent since the sequence of events is disrupted by the use of flashbacks or asides; the story does unravel in the expected order, but it is frequently broken into so that the reader is hard-pressed to appreciate its continuity.

In the broadest terms, the novel is in three parts. Of these the first takes the narrative from the dice-throwing scene through the robbery and the expulsion of Cava to culminate with the shooting of Esclavo (whose real name is Arana). The second part is rather less dramatic, dealing with the cover-up, and the

Alberto but has a g...
championing the cause of Esclavo. With that
banishment to the provinces the novel ends, save for a brief but
important epilogue.

The first and second parts are more or less comparable in size
and structure: each is composed of eight chapters which, in turn,
are (in all but one case) composites of shorter passages. These
last I shall refer to below as sections, using Arabic numerals to
identify them (and to contrast with the Roman numerals
employed for the chapters in the printed text). The sections are
marked off from one another by spacing and, much more
interestingly, by changes in the writing which involve a shift in
the perspective and a change in the author's stance. This may be
illustrated by a detailed examination of the first two chapters of
the novel, that is, roughly fifty pages of text. I shall examine the
various sections one by one, in their order of appearance,
pointing out some of the main elements of narrative content, the
technical and stylistic features and showing how the author
deliberately confronts his reader with puzzles. The brief
summary of the story which was made above should give the
reader of this Critical Guide sufficient orientation to follow the
section-by-section description which will now be given, without
totally undermining the author's strategy of covert information.
It is obviously advisable to keep the text close at hand at this
point, for easy cross-reference.

STRUCTURE AND THE ROLE OF THE AUTHOR

Chapter I, section 1 has the *perros* throwing dice to determine
who is to be the thief of the examination paper. Cava is selected
and sets out on his mission, which turns out to be successful save

for the broken window. The reader's entry to this taut spell of action is immediate. The development of the episode is particularly swift and compelling, but within these first four pages the author also describes the location, and identifies the participants by their (descriptive) nicknames, establishing the authority of Jaguar, and alluding to the fate of Cava, a *serrano* who is like the vicuña ('ese animal exclusivo de la sierra', p. 13) and is bound to return to the mountains. There is nothing stylistic to remark upon in all this: the author is an omniscient third-person narrator and his devices are traditional for that style.[7] In terms of the narrative itself, this is the fictive present, the time of the boys' life in the academy, which we shall live with them for all but the final pages of the novel.

With section 2 there comes the first disjunction; by this I mean that no obvious thread of a thematic, chronological or stylistic kind links the sections to one another. Instead of dialogue in the present with narration in preterites and imperfects (as in section 1), these last tenses are now used to flashback to a narrative past in the life of one Richi. The episode tells of his arrival in Lima, a timid, unhappy and perhaps over-protected child, alienated from his father. This flashback, including snippets of dialogue, is related to the present time of the narrative by its opening words: 'Ha olvidado...'. It seems reasonable at this early stage in the book to suppose that Richi is one of the Leoncio Prado pupils, possibly one who has already been identified, and that, paradoxically, what is said to have been forgotten ('Ha olvidado...') in fact constitutes the recollections of a present pupil. (The explicit identification of Richi with Esclavo is delayed until section 10, p. 47.)

We may note several contrasts with the opening section. To begin with, the author, while still omniscient and still third-person narrator, is no longer distanced from the action. He writes for Richi as much as about him, like a spokesman whose

[7] The ensuing discussion assumes some familiarity with terms such as 'authorial omniscience'. While these terms have become part of the normal language of literary criticism, it may be helpful to refer the reader to, for example, Wayne Booth, *The Rhetoric of Fiction* (Chicago: U.P., 1961), where they are defined in full.

[...which seems to]

the narrative, these words a[...]

obituary. Furthermore, of all the cadets, Esclavo is least able to stand up for himself, and it is therefore quite appropriate that the author should appear to be his spokesman, allowing the privilege of speaking for themselves only to those boys who will stand the test of survival. In keeping with this personalized third-person narrative, passages of dialogue are embedded into the broader framework of recollection, much as, later on, the thoughts of Alberto will be built into the sections which are focused on him.

A more general contrast with section 1, and a more obvious one, arises from the defusing of the tension that was conveyed in the opening section. Richi's recollections have none of the dynamism and latent aggression which pervade the opening section of the novel.

Section 3 opens with a monologue, quickly identified as coming from Alberto. Omniscient authorial commentary intervenes and so the pattern continues, the one style alternating with the other, for a good part of this section. However, this time the predominant tense used is the present. Also we should note that there are some equivocal passages in which events appear to be recorded as part of the direct experience of Alberto as much as they are the clinical record of the narrator, for example:

> Alberto vuelve a oír más fuerte (¿qué le pasa a este cadete?) y esta vez reaccionan su cuerpo y su espíritu, alza la cabeza, su mirada distingue...los muros de la Prevención...imagina su nombre en la lista de castigo, su corazón late alocado, siente pánico...(p.18)

For all the apparent confusion of Alberto's thoughts, they betray a resourceful personality capable of intelligent self-protection. Alberto is taxed by the fact that he lacks the necessary money to gain access both to the stolen examination questions and to the prostitute, Pies Dorados, of whose activities the boys like to boast. The monologue which begins section 3 is important for its content, but it is more remarkable for the diffuse manner in which it is presented. The passage provides a mass of references and allusions to factors which will only be clarified and whose relative importance can only be appreciated at a later stage in the book—the rôle of the pornographic stories, that of the boy's errant father, that of the prostitute, for example.

In general this long section tells a good deal about habit and hierarchy in the Leoncio Prado. At one point Alberto is caught straying from his guard duty, by Lt Huarina; when the latter angrily sends Alberto back to his post, the author seems to assert his control (pp.19-20). He has Alberto turn to face the barrack blocks, uses the chance to describe the compound and, under the guise of Alberto's recollection, tells the reader of the Director's speech which had justified the layout of the compound in terms of seniority. The Director's grandiose conception is promptly let down by the onset of another monologue, which deals with the problem of Alberto's bootlaces.

In time, the interplay of monologue and authorial observation subsides and the author predominates, the form of narration thus becoming substantially the same as that of section 1. Alberto has a lengthy encounter with Esclavo, whose defencelessness and dependence on Alberto are made clear; it is Esclavo who provides the money in exchange for Alberto's promise to write some love letters for him. The equivocal passages of third-person narration, to which I referred earlier, are those points at which the narrator seems to be closest to a particular character, as if only a linguistic convention barred him from assuming the perspective of that character. If one imagines the author as a cameraman, then these are the episodes which he records pointing his camera, as it were, over Alberto's shoulder.

Alberto is the main character once again in section 4 but the

new room.

> Le pareció más grande que la otra y
> evidentes: su dormitorio estaría más alejado del de sus
> padres y, como esta casa tenía un jardín interior,
> probablemente lo dejarían criar un perro. (p.29)

The detachment of the author in this second flashback contrasts with the closeness of the first (section 2). It contrasts far more pointedly with the intensely personal episode which follows. This (section 5) is the first of Boa's monologues. Boa was mentioned on the very first page of the novel, alluded to later by Alberto ('al bruto del Boa', p.20), but has otherwise been disregarded hitherto. Even now, in this, the first of a series of monologues by Boa, the perceptions recorded are really those of a collective consciousness of the cadets rather than those of one character; Boa's name appears frequently, but embedded in the comments of other cadets. Boa's function is unique and will justify special consideration later in this study. Compared with the relatively refined manner of Alberto, Boa's contributions to our impression of life in the academy are crude and visceral, given to violent and coarse sentiment, and conveyed in truncated syntax and vulgar colloquialisms. This effect is, of course, deliberate.

In a sense, the events recounted in section 5 (the rape and subsequent killing of a hen) are incidental to the main course of the plot. By dwelling on the distasteful details of this episode, and compounding the experience with the excursions of Boa's fantasy, Vargas Llosa achieves an extremely condensed and impressive picture of one of the characteristic escapades of the cadets in the Leoncio Prado. The denseness of the impression is reflected in the difficulty the passage presents to the reader; it is a monologue which has no narrative cushioning, no point of reference outside its protagonist. Note the contrasts made possible by the use of Boa to conclude the first chapter, full of personal fire and emphasis on the physical. With the opening of Chapter II the reader experiences an abrupt change of mood and style.

The start of the second chapter is a dispassionate documentary; it consists of a brief, generalized description which is purely authorial and contains not so much as a mention of an individual cadet. Throughout the second chapter (sections 6 to 11) the scenes are in the hands of the omniscient narrator, but only occasionally is he so clinically observant as in section 6. Dialogue turns the focus of attention to one individual after another, and occasionally the narrator draws closer to the personal viewpoint of a particular character. It is Alberto who is prominent in section 7 and, by virtue of his fragmentary monologues (e.g. p.42), to some degree also in section 8. Section 10 takes us back to the time of the initiation of Esclavo, obliquely identifies him with the Ricardo of section 2, shows the *perros*' introduction to the violent competitiveness of the Leoncio Prado, and explains the need for solidarity in defence, which led to the formation of the Circle.

But no sooner has Vargas Llosa clarified one question of identity than he creates another, one which is both more troublesome and more significant. On page 52 there begins a number of brief intervening monologues:

Ni fue tan grave como decían, ni como me pareció entonces...ni se puede comparar ese mes con los otros domingos de consigna, ni se puede...

With what character should the reader associate these words? Stoicism or bravado on the part of Esclavo (remember the epigraph to part one of the novel: 'On joue les héros...')?[8] Possibly, except that by this stage in the proceedings, Esclavo has receded from the foreground. Furthermore, this is an expression of someone's ability to cope and nowhere else is there

[8]'People play the hero because they are cowards, and the saint because they are wicked; they play at being murderers because they are dying to kill the next man, they play because they are born liars.'

The next

(p.54) ca......
passage in 5. Finally, the fact that secti...
reported statement by Jaguar implies that the previous thoughts
might, in fact, have been his:

Me das asco—dijo Jaguar—. No tienes dignidad.

Eres un esclavo.

In short, the sources of these interventions are obscure. This
kind of conscious ambiguity is both unsettling and
controversial; in due course we shall see how a particular case of
deliberately hidden identity has annoyed several critics.

Chapter II ends in the examination room as Gamboa
discovers the questions have been passed to Alberto. Esclavo
owns up and loses his weekend leave. It is this event which will
precipitate his revelation that Cava was the thief, and thereafter
lead to his apparent murder. (Coincidentally, it will also bring
Alberto into contact with Teresa.)

Compared with that of the first chapter, the course of the
second is simple and undisturbed. Throughout, the dominant
viewpoint is that of the narrator, and the style, therefore, is
comparatively consistent. The whole of the chapter is set in the
school. The events proceed chronologically save for the
flashback in section 10, although the rate of progress is, of
course, irregular. It is as if Vargas Llosa were here reverting to a
more traditional way of writing, filling in information which he
chose to deny his readers at the outset. The justification, he
would argue, is that life itself is not experienced in neatly
ordered chronological episodes; therefore the reader should be
made to experience the world of the novel in a similar manner.

The City, which faded from sight in the last chapter, comes
into its own in the following pages. The reader accompanies

Esclavo, Jaguar and, increasingly, Alberto in sorties from the Leoncio Prado which, in the case of the first two cadets, are also temporal flashbacks. Overwhelmingly, it is Alberto who has experience in the fictive present, both in and out of school. As before, the author wastes no opportunity for pointed contrast between sections; among the contrasts drawn may be those of style (sections 13-14), of dramatic tension (15-16), of personality (15-16) or of theme. This last contrast sometimes involves an irony bordering on cynicism, as for example in the juxtaposition of sections 23 and 24 (p.93): from the devout and protective arms of his mother, Alberto is transported to a discussion of and a physical encounter with the prostitute, who concludes:

'A lo mejor eres un santito de a deveras...Echate' (p.97)

The most intriguing device to follow the sample of techniques and styles I have noted already, is the introduction of a series of unidentified, section-length monologues, which begin with section 12. How is the reader to identify the person behind these monologues? Alberto has been as prominent as any character so far and one might be forgiven for taking the narrator's 'yo' in section 12 to refer to him. Certainly the style seems to eliminate Boa. (In any case, we are to see in retrospect, Boa has no existence outside the college.) The monologue reveals an unpretentious and unsophisticated interest in a girl called Teresa, an interest of a kind which might fit with what we know of the character of Esclavo, except that the family picture does not match his. A reason for discounting Alberto would be that in the days before he entered the academy he has been located in Miraflores, and prior to that in Breña; Bellavista, which is the background for the events of this monologue, is near the dockland on the other side of the city. In any case, are not the simple style and rough habits of the narrator at variance with our image of Alberto? And who, too, is Higueras?

At what is still, after all, an early stage in the novel, the identification of the monologuist has to be kept in abeyance; even a certain amount of detective work with the aid of a city map will not yield results.[9] At the end of the book the identity in

[9]Early editions by Seix Barral did include a map of Lima.

Whether the

of Boa's (section 13), but one

physical assertiveness of Jaguar. For the identity is his: Jaguar turns out to be the greatest impostor of them all and sections 12 and 13 present pictures of, respectively, his private (city) self and his public (academy) persona. Higueras, it turns out, is a petty criminal, a friend of Jaguar both before and after his college days.

The techniques outlined above are reiterated to varying degrees in the ensuing chapters, the city and the school vying for prominence. It is not necessary for us to consider the deployment of these techniques in continuing detail, for we already have enough of a sample upon which to base some generalized description. The first part of the novel ends with the death of Esclavo; the second has rather less dramatic pace, exploring the reactions of the main cadets and of Lt Gamboa, as also the moral issues involved. As before, it is possible to describe each section according to the predominant character(s) in it, often related to a particular perspective on the action; in an informal way this is what was done above, in some detail, for Chapter I. We can mark the various sections as follows:

Type A: Alberto. Sometimes his personal viewpoint is taken, at others we observe the action beside him, with rather more detachment. The rôle of the narrator in this is complicated and inclined to change frequently; however, the narrator's presence is usually felt by the reader.

Type B: Boa. The action perceived entirely through his solitary monologues (and often with himself as a prominent participant in this action). The perceptions are sensual and are not presented in a very rational manner. While Alberto's monologues are located in context and often have the air of reported thoughts, Boa's are hermetic and free. The narrator (*qua* narrator) is absent. Also the monologuist's audience is remote or imprecise, so that these monologues have almost a therapeutic quality for Boa, rather than being addressed to others.

Type C: The academy cadets as viewed *en masse* by an impartial, third-person narrator (e.g. the concluding section of Part I).

Type E: Esclavo. Flashbacks normally, the most striking ones with 'Ha olvidado...' in the opening sentence. A parenthetical (E) indicates the viewpoint of Esclavo when not so heralded. A narrator is always present, though less obtrusive in E than in (E).

Type G: Gamboa. Always observed with detachment by the third-person of the narrator, though not without occasional privileged access to Gamboa's thoughts.

Type J: Jaguar. The view is from him (that is, the reader views the action from Jaguar's perspective) in his monologues which, like those of Boa, deny the intervention of the narrator. However, unlike Boa's, these monologues are perfectly orderly reports of experiences which take place before he enters the academy. There is always a simple narrative thread. There are no excursions into fantasy, the tone is muted and sensitive, with something of the air of a confession. It is not hard to imagine a confidant for these monologues, perhaps Higueras. Note that Jaguar is a dominant participant in the action portrayed in various sections where the focus is on him, but that his perspective is adopted only in these monologues.

Type T: Teresa. The action observed alongside her, usually in a detached way, but with a degree of closeness on page 79 and more importantly in the section

learns of Esclavo's

a section to a particular char... of classification; a scene may be Gamboa's or Teresa's as much by virtue of thematic focus as by virtue of assuming their particular perspective. But for all these provisos, the classification does allow us to give an outline of the way in which the different characters lose or acquire prominence for the reader. The full pattern is this:

	Chapter	Sections
Part I:	I	C E A A B
	II	C A C C (E) C
	III	J B A B (E)
	IV	A T A T A A
	V	J C E C A A
	VI	(E) A
	VII	J B A B E
	VIII	C

	Chapter	Section
Part II:	I	B A J A E B A B (E)
	II	J C J C
	III	B T J A B A
	IV	B J A J G
	V	B G J C
	VI	A J A
	VII	G J A
	VIII	C G A
Epilogue:		G A J

On the above count Alberto has twenty-three sections, Jaguar thirteen and Boa twelve. In addition to these totals we must make allowances for the prominence of these three cadets in the impartial, type C, scenes. Alberto is undoubtedly pre-eminent. Jaguar and Boa present an interesting contrast. Boa exists only as a member of the cadet society within the academy; although his monologues might themselves in theory occur outside the college, they deal exclusively with intra-mural experiences. Jaguar, on the other hand, occupies the scene on many occasions within the college, but his monologues, equal in number to those of Boa, deal only with experiences outside it; I have already suggested that Jaguar's may be taken as confessions to a friend. In narrative terms, Boa neither pre-exists nor survives the academy; Esclavo, of necessity, does not survive it. All of which puts both Jaguar and Alberto firmly into the position of main characters. They are, also, the only two cadets to feature in the Epilogue, which deals with their experiences after they have left the college.

For technical reasons, the final section of the Epilogue deserves close attention. Jaguar has left school and is telling his friend *el flaco Higueras* about Teresa, once his childhood sweetheart, whom he has recently met again since leaving the Leoncio Prado. It is, of course, only now that the unidentified monologues can conclusively (though by now somewhat less improbably) be attributed to Jaguar; not only does he talk about the Teresa he knew before school days but he refers back to the time he fought for her on the beach (already enacted on pp.273-4), while she for her part clarifies the early reference to Bellavista. While he is resolving the puzzle of the monologues, Vargas Llosa also clarifies the importance of Teresa. I mentioned the interest shown by some unidentified person in Teresa when discussing section 12 (above p.32), the first of (what we now know to be) the Jaguar monologues. On reading the Epilogue, it can be assumed that this is the same Teresa who was loved by Esclavo, who provided the motive for his denunciation of Cava, the examination thief, and who therefore indirectly led to Esclavo's death. Moreover, Alberto trifles with the affections of this same Teresa, eventually to drop her in favour of the at-m, apart from the obvious use of the vicuña. Vargas Llo

tractions of more middle-class girls.

idénticos, las veredas desiguales, el polvo suspendido en el aire.

(*c*) —Nada. Se quedó mirándome con unos ojazos asustados, como si yo le diera miedo.
—No creo—dijo el flaco Higueras—. Eso no creo. Algo tuvo que decirte. Al menos hola o qué ha sido de tu vida, o cómo estás; en fin, algo.

(*b*) No, no le había dicho nada hasta que él habló de nuevo. Sus primeras palabras, al abordarla, habían sido precipitadas, imperiosas: 'Teresa, ¿te acuerdas de mí? ¿Cómo estás?' (*d*) El Jaguar sonreía, para mostrar que nada había de sorprendente en ese encuentro, que se trataba de un episodio banal, chato y sin misterio. Pero esa sonrisa le costaba un esfuerzo muy grande y en su vientre había brotado, como esos hongos de silueta blanca y cresta amarillenta que nacen repentinamente en las maderas húmedas, un malestar insólito, que invadía ahora sus piernas, ansiosas de dar un paso atrás, adelante o a los lados, sus manos que querían zambullirse en los bolsillos o tocar su propia cara; y, extrañamente, su corazón albergaba un miedo animal, como si esos impulsos, al convertirse en actos, fueran a desencadenar una catástrofe.
—¿Y tú qué hiciste?—dijo el flaco Higueras.
—Le dije otra vez: 'hola Teresa. ¿No te acuerdas de mí?' Y entonces ella dijo:

—Claro que sí. No te había reconocido.

El respiró. Teresa la sonreía, le tendía la mano. El contacto fue muy breve, apenas sintió el roce de los dedos de la muchacha, pero todo su cuerpo se serenó y des-aparecieron el malestar, la agitación de sus miembros, y el miedo.

The passage represents two encounters at different times and in different places. After Higueras's opening question (*a*), the description of Teresa's attitude and surroundings, which might have taken the form of a recollection by Jaguar, is instead given as the observation of the third-person narrator, as if present at that earlier encounter (*b*). Jaguar's following words (*c*) bring us back again to the true present of his conversation with Higueras. By the third line of the following paragraph (*d*) the earlier scene with Teresa is being portrayed as present again, this time by a third-person narrator close to Jaguar. So the scenes shift from the 'true' present of Jaguar-Higueras to the other present of Jaguar-Teresa, with the narrator witnessing both. At this passage's points of closest fusion, an utterance in one scene is perceived in the other and creates an intimacy between Teresa and Higueras, who were in fact separated by time and space (see *3*, p.420). Teresa's last 'sí' almost seems to answer Higueras's question. Note also the ambivalence of the words italicised below:

—¿Hace como cinco años, no?—decía Teresa—. Quizá más.

—Seis—dijo el Jaguar; bajó un poco la voz:—Y tres meses.

—La vida se pasa volando—dijo Teresa—. Pronto estaremos viejos.

Se rio y el Jaguar pensó: 'ya es una mujer.'

—¿Y tu mamá?—dijo ella.

—¿No sabías? Se murió.

—Ese era un buen pretexto—dijo el flaco Higueras—. ¿Qué hizo ella?

—Se paró—repuso el Jaguar; tenía un cigarrillo entre los labios y miraba el cono de humo denso que expulsaba su

boca; una de sus manos tamborilaba en

—Dijo: '¡qué pena! Pobrecita.'

—Ahí debiste besarla y decirle al Higueras. Era el momento.

—Sí—dijo el Jaguar—. Pobrecita.

Quedaron callados. Continuaron can manos en los bolsillos y la miraba dijo:

—Quería hablarte. Quiero decir, sabía dónde estabas.

—¡Ah!—dijo el flaco Higueras—.

—Sí—dijo el Jaguar; miraba el hu

—Sí—dijo Teresa—. Desde que n a Bellavista. Hace cuánto tiempo

—Quería pedirte perdón—dijo por lo de la playa, esa vez.

This narrative device has an effe often used in comedy, in which an from years or miles away, remon he goes about his life in the here use the technique of the *vasos* much more ambitiously in later he points out himself.[10] To Ha its purpose as follows:

Crear una ambigüedad, es unidad narrativa dos o más pos y lugares distintos, p episodio circulen de u mutuamente.

We have already seen, or *rros*, that Vargas Llosa is adopt and sustain a variety he is a linguistic craftsmar at least in the text that cor nor is there any experim Cortázar or Cabrera Inf

[10]In 'La estrategia narrativa 40-1.

boli
disti
cons
infor
critic
perm
book

to the novel's overall themes. We have seen that there are two first-person narrators, Jaguar and Boa; another quasi-first-person narrator is Alberto in his interior monologues. Together they may be thought of as internal to the action because they are narrator-actors. Of course, the author is in fact the real narrator behind all three, but he is on a different plane, external to the action, and the reader is often unaware of him; however, on occasions the author does also act as an overt narrator, in the omniscient accounts of the cadets together, in those of Teresa, of the officers, in many passages concentrating on Alberto, and in those portraying the feelings of Esclavo. There are, then, four narrative voices in all: Jaguar and Boa (both in first person but clearly differentiated by style), Alberto (first-person interior monologues), and the author (narrating in the third person). Sharon Magnarelli (26, p.36) goes so far as to claim that this fact is obliquely indicated in the very first word of the novel. Be that as it may, the fact of there being four narrators, only three of whom are also internal characters, is a further structural reason why Jaguar, Boa and Alberto can be described as the most important. The one cadet to whom considerable attention is given but who is not a narrator is Esclavo. We shall consider him first, only to conclude that he is primarily a device to set the drama in motion.

Esclavo's experiences before entry to the college are recorded in the reminiscences of the 'Ha olvidado...' passages. He fits the stereotype of the middle-class child who, having become estranged from his father, is brought up by a mother who proves to be over-solicitous. In view of her influence, and that of an aunt, his father feels he must be made a real man and sends him away to school. But, like an animal reared in captivity, he is poorly prepared to fend for himself in the wild—that is, in the Leoncio Prado Academy. Physically puny (p.36), he will be despised and therefore dubbed Esclavo by Jaguar (p.54), befriended by Alberto because of his defencelessness and inadequacy, and eventually sacrificed as part of a Darwinian struggle in which only the fittest survive. It is Jaguar who will remark that 'En el colegio todos friegan a todos, el que se deja se arruina.'

Esclavo's true identity is not acknowledged by the school or his peers until the time of his death (p.168). Note, too, that that death is made all the more poignant by one of the author's judicious pieces of organisation; the section which records the shooting follows immediately on another which recollects Esclavo's entry into the college. For dramatic effect, Vargas Llosa has the reader experience the expectations, apprehensions and hopes that are associated with starting life in the school only to shatter them cruelly and immediately (pp.150-168). I have already noted how Esclavo's death was presaged at the outset by the litany-like style of his recollections. All the foregoing tends to support Oviedo's suggestion (*6*, p.113) that narrative features mark off Esclavo in an exceptional way; nevertheless, distinctions of different kinds can also be ascribed to other characters (see *41*).

Critics were quick to suggest to the author, in the early sixties, that he was himself reflected in the character of Alberto, largely on the strength of the latter's intelligence and his literary persona. 'Yo no me reconozco absolutamente en Alberto', responded the author (*14*, p.76; see also p.79). In fact, in view of his comments to Harss (*4*, p.433) on the subject of his father, Vargas Llosa might be thought to have something in common with Ricardo Arana.

Joseph Sommers, in an interesting article, describes Ricardo thus:

> ...se presenta al lector como un clásico ejemplo en que predominan términos edípicos freudianos. Al juntar los fragmentos centrados en Ricardo, narrados en tercera

~~persons se conforma el retrato de un muchacho~~

self-sufficient. In the *macho* system of the Leoncio Prado his passivity and evasion of violent encounters are interpreted as weakness. According to Georg Rudolf Lind (*28*, p.64) Esclavo is a model example of a constant in Vargas Llosa's fiction: the solidarity of the group and the need of the individual to live by the group's tenets or otherwise become an outcast:

> Cuando el Esclavo se decide finalmente a un gesto espontáneo, su actuación contradice el código de honor reinante en el grupo: delata el robo de los exámenes y se hace soplón, excluyéndose así del círculo de sus camaradas. Su muerte...parece un castigo excesivo por la infracción de un código de tan restringida validez, limitado a cierto grupo de adolescentes. Sin embargo, su muerte ejerce un efecto purificador, y por eso, Vargas Llosa la ha colocado en el centro de la novela.

Similarly, Oviedo (*8*, p.350) classifies Esclavo in the same category as another of Vargas Llosa's creations, Pichula Cuéllar. Cuéllar is one of a group of upper-middle-class children who makes every effort to integrate into that group despite a physical disqualification: his manhood is in doubt because of accidental castration. Cuéllar is protagonist of a short novel entitled, significantly, *Los cachorros* and published in 1967.

Since Esclavo's death is the means of launching the drama, and thereby revealing the mettle of those who live and work in the Academy, it follows that the exploration of his own character is truncated precisely at the point at which the others begin to acquire a new depth of interest. Esclavo must inevitably be less rounded than the other characters and his value to the novel is to a great extent for the development of its plot, as a 'factor desencadenante' (*29*, p.95).

However vividly he may impinge on the consciousness of the reader, Boa is another limited character. Although, unlike Esclavo, he presumably survives his days in the Academy, we learn nothing of him afterwards, for he does not feature in the Epilogue. Nor do we know much at all about his past, apart from a passing reference to an alcoholic father. Boa's, then, is exclusively a college rôle, and perhaps he loses something of his credibility because of this; there is no doubt as to the impressive power of his monologues, which seem almost to buffet the reader through an inventory of the less agreeable activities of the cadets. The intensity of his episodes, and their presentation in such a striking and demanding style, to some extent draw the reader's attention to their form and therefore distance him from the action. It is a curious paradox that when the reader's human sensibilities are most stimulated, when the activities portrayed are most likely to provoke a response of distaste or revulsion in him, he becomes unusually conscious of the way this effect is being achieved by the author.

The author has admitted that Boa is a contrivance. In order to give a true picture of life in the college Vargas Llosa thought it necessary to present certain episodes which verged on the pornographic, or at least the sensational; the great risk, as he saw it, was that his portrayal of these unpleasant aspects might appear to be artificial and lose credibility:

> Yo lo intenté en la primera versión enorme de la novela, por medio de diálogos y descripciones puras. Las escenas de masturbación colectiva, por ejemplo; el episodio de la gallina...Resultaban irreales, por desmedidas, y su violencia gratuita...Después de una serie de pruebas y de ensayos encontré que la manera de amortiguar más estas escenas sin que además perdieran su carácter, así, definitorio, era por medio de una conciencia en movimiento...Así nació el Boa. (*4*, pp.436-7)

He describes Boa's episodes as the most 'trabajadas', the most carefully contrived and stylised; yet it was equally necessary to

...itself an unintelligent and irrational

the first part of the book. The form of these monologues is thus a crucial corollary of the experiences they seek to convey; the imperfect syntax provides a reading experience which is in a way analogous to the chaos of the impressions. Just as Boa is irrational, he is inarticulate: the limits of his reason and his language contrast violently with the corresponding strengths of Alberto. Boa is also nameless, that is to say that he is labelled with an animal category but not a civilian (or civilised) name. It is a feature which, curiously, he shares with Jaguar, who nevertheless does have an extra-collegiate existence in the novel. And it is a feature which invites comparisons with other animal imagery in the novel, a matter to which I shall return later.

Boa's animal nature and his linguistic limits make his contact with other cadets physical rather than verbal. Similarly, he has genuine affection for—and a real physical relationship with—his bitch Malpapeada (who also has no past). His relationship with her reveals both his underlying kindness and his inability to express it on a human level. There is, however, the time when he is moved to sympathy by the courage of Cava in the face of authority, despite racial prejudice against the *serrano*. In the end Boa defends Jaguar against the others and attempts to befriend him; but (because he is a different species?) he is rejected. Boa does not appear in the Epilogue nor is any reference made to him; he has served up till then as a kind of abstract cadet consciousness.

Es el personaje más instintivo de todos...Todas las manifestaciones de su interioridad están dadas exclusivamente en función del instinto...es su vínculo más

fuerte con el mundo y con los otros. (*4*, pp.431-2)
The whole business of Boa is all the more impressive when one
puts together on the one hand the knowledge that he is a
deliberate narrative device and, on the other, the onslaught on
the reader's feelings achieved in his monologues. For example:
a la embajadora debimos hacerle también el chajuí,
chajuá, hasta los perros se pusieron a aplaudir y los
suboficiales y los tenientes, no paren, sigan, pam-pam-
pam, y no le quiten los ojos al coronel, la embajadora y el
ministro se largan y a él se le torcerá de nuevo la cara y dirá
se creían muy vivos pero voy a barrer el suelo con ustedes,
pero se comenzó a reír, y el general Mendoza, y los
embajadores y los oficiales y los invitados, pam-pam-pam,
uy qué buenos somos todos, uy papacito, uy mamacita,
pam-pam-pam, todos somos leonciopradinos ciento por
ciento, viva el Perú cadetes, algún día la Patria nos llamará
y ahí estaremos, alto el pensamiento, firme el corazón,
'¿dónde está Gambarina para darle un beso en la boca?',
decía el Jaguar, 'quiero decir si quedó vivo después de
tanto contrasuelazo que le di', la mujer está llorando con
los aplausos, Malpapeada, la vida del colegio es dura y
sacrificada pero tiene sus compensaciones, lástima que el
Círculo no volviera a ser lo que era, el corazón me
aumentaba en el pecho cuando nos reuníamos los treinta
en el baño, el diablo se mete siempre en todo con sus
cachos peludos, qué sería que todos nos fregáramos por el
serrano Cava, que le dieran de baja, que nos dieran de baja
por un cochino vidrio, por tu santa madre no me metas los
dientes, Malpapeada, perra.

Alberto, 'individualizado, protagónico' (*29*, p.97) is a richly
but clearly portrayed character; the many sides of his personality
conveyed in a variety of ways are open to immediate and
unambiguous appreciation by the reader. Flashbacks provide a
full picture of his early family life: comfortably middle-class,
moving as finances permit from one suburb to another
(Miraflores, the most fashionable), economically secure,
enjoying games with childhood friends. It is a picture marred

only by the disagreements between his parents. His father, whom Alberto secretly admires, is a selfish womanizer,

convertible, una gran casa con piscina. Me casaré con Marcela y seré un don Juan. Iré todos los sábados a bailar al Grill Bolívar y viajaré mucho. Dentro de algunos años ni me acordaré que estuve en el Leoncio Prado. (p. 335)

Until this point the reader's sympathies have largely been on Alberto's side. He has shown courage (p.293), accusing Jaguar of making Esclavo's life a misery and revealing that Alberto himself was responsible for the denunciation of Jaguar. Though it does nothing for his image amongst his peers to do so, he has supported the defenceless Esclavo when alive (though that does not stop him from turning Esclavo's contact with Teresa to his own advantage). On the death of his friend, Alberto is genuinely remorseful however, and accepts alone the responsibility of speaking up about the incident. He tries to bring out what he believes is the truth but is not strong enough to resist being blackmailed into silence by the authorities. He thus compromises himself and only Gamboa will listen; but he, too, will be silenced by the military machine in a different way.

That Alberto should turn from resourceful opportunist to cynic is scarcely surprising in the circumstances. Of the novel as a whole Escobar (*8*, p.131) writes:

Ni jóvenes ni adultos son capaces de asumir la decisión que los conforme como aspirantes de la dignidad a que naturalmente pretende el ser humano: pero todos los personajes aparentan serlo, inventan razones, se autoconvencen o dejan persuadir, y, en ese sentido, la calidad común que los vincula no es otra que la de ser impostores de sí mismos.

Before dismissing him as a callous self-seeker, we might
nevertheless do well to reflect on whether Alberto's intelligence
has not allowed him to draw conclusions for himself not unlike
those of Escobar. Alberto certainly does not emerge as noble,
for he gives in to self-interest and acts all the while in the
knowledge of the secure and comfortable future ahead of him.
That Vargas Llosa should have him act in that way may indicate
that the author has a depressingly negative view of human
nature, but it may equally be a realistic one.

Alberto is something of a hero until he fails the final test,
succumbing to the pressure of the system. The reader is won
over by Alberto's resourcefulness—witness his ability to adapt
to the Leoncio Prado using his quick-wittedness or his eloquence
or playing the fool. Also engaging is the inadvertent humour of
his situation, the hollowness of his adolescent sexual bravado
compared with his total lack of real experience. Not least among
his persuasive attributes is his command of language; this is the
particular mask which Alberto uses to project a persona in the
academy.

All the cadets fake rôles under peer-group pressure. Alberto
assumes his—'Poeta'—by writing love letters or (ironically)
pornographic stories for the others, further confirming his
verbal skill in his confrontations with the officers and his ease in
talking to people outside. He is articulate yet ultimately
superficial; other cadets (Boa is the clearest example) feel more
acutely but lack the verbal dexterity of Alberto to express it. If
language is a mask for Alberto then it hides his true self; in the
end the mask is removed and the reader, seeing his true nature in
full, switches allegiance from the character to whom he has felt
closest throughout.

I have already referred to the fact that Alberto is present in
several narrative modes. The third-person episodes, especially
the flashbacks, are largely objective accounts by an impartial
and all-knowing narrator. Those third-person accounts which
render episodes in the college are less objective and in them are
often embedded Alberto's thoughts in a subjective stream of

consciousness; see, for example, p.136, or p.127 as follows:

Alberto no puede advertirle que se aproxima el suboficial: éste no le quita los ojos de encima y avanza

semanas, no debí comenzar nunca a escribir novelitas, no debí salir de Miraflores, no debí conocer a Teresa ni amarla.'

In the previous chapter I wrote of how the perspective can shift subtly from the objective third person towards the first person of Alberto. Sometimes his thoughts are reported in a Flaubertian manner: 'What if he were to...He might discover that...and then there was the...' More originally, Vargas Llosa allows a verbal trigger to spark off a loose association in Alberto's mind; and from this he launches into what Silva Cáceres (*3*, p.419), in what was probably the best of the early reviews, calls 'diálogo interior'. This is a dialogue which may be a real one recalled by Alberto, or may be wholly imagined by him, or indeed may be a mixture of the two types or a collage of dialogues from different times and places. The following extract (p.253) provides an illustration:

La marcha hacia las aulas, en cambio, es un gran ruido marcial, equilibrado y exacto que va disminuyendo lentamente hasta desaparecer. 'Ya se habrán dado cuenta, Teresita, el poeta no ha venido, Arróspide ha escrito mi nombre en el parte de ausentes, cuando sepan se sortearán a ver quién me pega, se pasarán papeles y mi padre dirá mi apellido en el fango, en la página policial de los periódicos, tu abuelo y tu bisabuelo morirían de impresión, nosotros fuimos siempre y en todo los mejores y tú te pudres en la mugre, Teresita, nos escaparemos a Nueva York y nunca volveremos al Perú, ahora ya comenzaron las clases y deben estar mirando mi carpeta.' Alberto da un paso atrás cuando ve al teniente Ferrero acercarse al calabozo. La puerta metálica se abre silenciosamente.

In short, we have introspective, personal insights together with detached description, all inclined to complex intertwining. This rich variety of presentation is another formal reason why Alberto seems to be the central character. José Miguel Oviedo (*6*, pp.111-12) says that this makes Alberto successively 'actor, testigo, cómplice, juez de la acción'. But for him, too, it emphasises the moral duplicity of Alberto's nature.

A third-person narrative does not simply suggest (however deceptively) that the narrator is giving an objective picture of events, it also suggests that our assessment of characters portrayed in this way is more reliable. Yet there are constant signs that Alberto is devious and dishonest and these serve to undermine that reliability; and since Alberto is spoken of, and a spokesman for himself (indirectly), we have here a formal feature which parallels the duplicity of his nature.

That two-sideness is not limited to Alberto; it is, of course, one of the novel's major themes: everyone is an impostor, 'on joue les héros parce qu'on est lâche...' Jaguar is the prime case. He is presented in two diametrically opposing facets, one of them covert; formal, linguistic means are used to portray the two sides of his personality. In particular, language functions as a personal mask for Alberto; he uses it as if playing a game, in an automatic, almost profligate fashion. In general the author uses language as a means of covering different aspects of the characters' personalities. When he, as it were, dramatises the role of language in this way, its own reliability is called into question, and one becomes aware of how it can be used to govern one's perceptions of what is true.

Mario Benedetti, the Uruguayan writer, observes that the Epilogue makes a conclusive statement on the character of Alberto:

El categórico y justiciero epílogo le muestra reintegrado a su clase, a su lujoso Miraflores, a la hipocresía, en fin. El

────── is both pessimistic and deterministic (see, especially, *30*). In Alberto's case, circumstances do get the upper hand and ultimately he exercises his personal will only to conform. But it can be argued (and has been, e.g. *31*, part II) that in other major characters redeeming features play a significant part.

It is by means of Alberto that Vargas Llosa gives his clearest statement about the structure of Peruvian society. The family, which has given rise to Alberto's ambivalence, has also sown in him the seeds of class-consciousness; one is increasingly aware that Alberto acts in response to social conventions. He begins and ends comfortably in the middle class, where the man abuses his wife and at the same time pays lip-service to the sanctity of marriage. The complexity of narrative emphasises the confusions and contradictions of Alberto's situation: the stream of consciousness brings feelings of guilt, fear and hope into the arena of present experience. To some degree his weakness has its roots in an unhappy home and he can only be understood with reference to it and the class it represents.

Having raised the subject of class it is natural to turn to Teresa before completing the survey of the main cadets. She is scornfully referred to by Marcela at the end as a 'huachafa'; was Alberto never embarrassed to be seen out with Teresa? (p.333). The answer is no: at the time, what bothered him was that he was not like her, not of her background. All the same it is clear that from early on (p.136) his attitude to her has been patronising.

In a very different way, Teresa is a victim of her family circumstances; her parents have left her in the care of an aunt, not through lack of love but through hardship. As evidence of poverty she has to beg a shower in a neighbour's house, borrow a ribbon from a friend. She is essentially passive, accepting her abandonment, putting up with maltreatment from her aunt and insults from men in the street. She is flattered when Alberto reveals his interest in her by questioning her about her contact with Esclavo. Esclavo is her social equal or, in her own words, 'el muchacho que vive en la esquina' (p.137).

Vargas Llosa manages a touching episode (pp.229-35) when Teresa anxiously awaits a visit by Alberto, and ends by realising that already he is moving away from her. Alberto will go on to socially higher and more appropriate things; Esclavo lacks the self-assurance to make anything of the relationship and while he is alive it remains an impossible ideal for him. But Jaguar will see his childhood love through to the end by marrying her. The transition from pages 138 to 139 is another interesting one. It takes us from a chapter which ends with Alberto declaring to Teresa that he is in love with her, to the beginning of one in which the unidentified *yo* (Jaguar) tells of how he used to hope to say hello to her in the street, to have tentative conversations with her, and recounts his vivid recollections of her appearance and mannerisms. The fact that this is the same Teresa is slightly obscured by use of her full name when in contact with Alberto and the abbreviated 'Tere' with Jaguar. Given also that Alberto's Teresa is, or was, Esclavo's, the coincidence with a third cadet seems far-fetched, especially since Jaguar is appparently unaware of the Alberto-Teresa-Esclavo connection, as are they of his own with the girl. It is sufficiently improbable for the reader to wonder if this is another girl, and when he discovers she is in fact the same he may find it too unbelievable, too artificial. This is a point raised by several critics (see, e.g. *6*, p.103; *9*, p.65) and one answered repeatedly by the author. He does not necessarily deny the weakness, but points out that Gallagher (*44*, p. 137) regards Teresa as an asset, for she acts as a kind of social barometer for the three boys; this had been the author's aim (*8*, p.54). However, a fundamental divergence of outlook underlies the intention of Vargas Llosa on the one hand and the defence provided by Gallagher on the other. The latter acknowledges that Teresa

, ... iuisa o

, ..., silu unica y exclusivamente que la forma en que
esa anécdota está encarnada fracasó, se frustró (*19*, p.105).

Clearly the author's own criterion is not the only one and
there is a case for saying that *La ciudad y los perros* is in general
a more obviously artificial novel than he would like to admit.
But by his own criterion he does, I think, fail with Teresa. It is
not that she lacks credibility as a character, although she is
representative of a type as much as she is an individual; she fails
him as a device because the device itself depends on our fully
accepting that this Teresa is the one Jaguar also loves. And the
difficulty in accepting this may partly depend in turn on the
credibility of Jaguar.

'No creo que exista el diablo pero el Jaguar me hace dudar a
veces' (p.141). These words are judiciously placed immediately
after Jaguar's *alter ego* has given a disarmingly innocent and
sincere account of Tere: it is the same account to which I
referred a while ago. The force of the contrast, within the same
personality, is nevertheless lost for the reader, who at this stage
cannot have concluded that *yo* and Jaguar are one and the same
person. The violence of the contradiction brought about in this
sudden transition from Jekyll to Hyde can be appreciated only
with hindsight. This and other examples demonstrate that *La
ciudad y los perros* is a novel to re-read; the revelations of the
Epilogue, above all, are such as to cast doubt on our reading of
all that went before. Is it, then, a matter of perversity to
withhold the means of understanding till the end? And what, in
any case, are the characteristics of each of Jaguar's two

personalities?

In the academy, Jaguar embodies the myths of *machismo* and physical prowess; in this he is the antithesis of Esclavo, a fact which Jaguar himself indirectly acknowledges when giving Ricardo his nickname. Jaguar is feared by the other cadets and dominates them fully by superior force, snarling at any threats to his territorial authority. Alberto is the only cadet who dares to stand up to Jaguar and in doing so earns his respect but not his friendship. Jaguar respects his wish to avenge his friend Esclavo. Apart from the dubious allegiance of Boa, Jaguar is friendless throughout, but never more so than just before the college episode is drawn to a close. Jaguar despises the other cadets for their failure to honour their own code of conduct, for their cowardice. Now they are turning against him: Arróspide has incited the others to a chorus of 'soplón' directed at Jaguar, like the humiliating chants they engage in in their French classes; Alberto, first assuring himself of his own immunity from the accusation, joins in the chorus, and they all pounce on Jaguar and Boa, the only one still loyal to him. All, that is, except Alberto, who protects himself: 'El se había dejado caer en el lecho, para evitar los golpes, los brazos levantados como un escudo' (p.311).

In the end, Jaguar no longer communicates with any of them, even Boa:

> La vida era otra vez normal. Pero todos sabían que entre ellos había un exiliado... 'Parece que fuera él quien nos hace hielo', pensaba Alberto, 'él quien estuviera castigando a la sección.' (p.316)

When the solidarity of the *perros* is broken and Jaguar has lost their respect, he comments that now he is in a better position to understand Esclavo. Signs of his underlying softness begin to emerge; accused of all manner of evil, he responds only that his mother used to complain in a similar way. Yet so strong has the readers' sense of revulsion from him been that he scarcely wins any sympathy once ostracised; from parts I and II he emerges as a dogged adherent to his principles whose reward is to be a life of obscurity. In both these respects he is like Gamboa.

Prior to entry into the acad

...ado. Having concluded, as Dorfman has it (*8*, p.150), that life is a jungle, Jaguar behaves as a noble beast; if the rest are like animals then it becomes a matter of which animal is strongest, will not be beaten, will meet violence with violence. So successfully does he assert himself once inside that he even escapes the humiliating initiation ceremonies (p.49). Jaguar enters the academy with an advantage of sorts over the other cadets. He is the only one to have had direct experience of the adult world; for the others such experience has been mediated by parents.

Let us now look at the question of Jaguar's presumed guilt of Esclavo's murder. For Sommers the matter is not in doubt; because of this he is able to see irony in Jaguar's progress towards respectability contrasted with his guilt of the ultimate of moral crimes, murder (*27*, p.90). However, that Jaguar is guilty is by no means proven. To begin with, when Alberto denounces Jaguar as murderer, the author follows with a section which obliquely demonstrates that Jaguar not Alberto is the better person for the innocent Teresa (pp.253-60). Secondly, when Gamboa accuses Jaguar of murder the latter repeatedly denies it and becomes angry that he should have been both accused and betrayed by a fellow cadet (pp.268-72). At once Vargas Llosa switches the narrative to relate how, in the past, Jaguar found his beloved Teresa had given him up for another boy, how he was severely chastised as a result, how he broke away from home to live with Higueras. With hindsight it appears that the author is trying to emphasize the injustice and the extent of Jaguar's suffering, implying that the accusation of murder is part of that

injustice. Later, realising that there is to be a cover-up, Alberto
threatens:

>...cuando salga del colegio, iré a decirle a la policía que
eres un asesino.
>
>Estás loco—dijo el Jaguar, sin exaltarse—Sabes muy bien
que no he matado a nadie. Todos saben que el Esclavo se
mató por accidente. Sabes muy bien eso, soplón. (p.303)

And later in the same confrontation, Jaguar seems to show that
he was unaware of the fact that Esclavo had betrayed Cava.
Effectively this deprives Alberto of the motive upon which he
had built his deduction that Jaguar was guilty:

>Jura que no sabías que el Esclavo denunció a Cava. Jura
por tu madre. Di que se muera mi madre si lo sabía. Jura.
>
>—Mi madre ya se murió—dijo el Jaguar—pero no sabía.
>
>—Jura si eres hombre.
>
>—Juro que no sabía.
>
>—Creí que sabías y que por eso lo habías matado—dijo
Alberto—Si de veras no sabías, me equivoqué.
Discúlpame, Jaguar. (p.306)

The Epilogue is equivocal on the subject of Jaguar's guilt. In
its opening section Gamboa, leaving the academy, is followed by
Jaguar at a distance of a few yards. Gamboa stops to question
Jaguar about a note which he has been given. The text of this
note seems to consist of a confession by Jaguar. Jaguar chooses
to approach Gamboa, not the captain who is still a college
official; he is concerned to reinstate himself in the eyes of his
peers and turns instinctively to the officer he most respects:

>¿Ha visto las paredes de los baños? 'Jaguar soplón, Jaguar
amarillo', por todas partes. Y yo *lo* hice por ellos, es lo
peor. ¿Qué podía ganar yo?...Todo lo hice por la sección.
>(p.324)

The italicized *lo* (the italics are mine) might refer to anything and
everything, and Gamboa's rejoinder proves nothing:

>No es verdad—dijo Gamboa—está mintiendo. Si la
opinión de sus compañeros le importa tanto ¿prefiere que
sepan que es un asesino?

Shortly after, Gamboa puts the question baldly to Jaguar. Why did he kill Esclavo? Th

...be easier to resurrect
Arana than to persuade the authorities to change their mind.
Gamboa enjoins Jaguar to forget his confession and to make
sure that Esclavo's death serves some good purpose. He tears up
the confession and with it the telegram announcing the birth of
his daughter. As Jaguar pieces them together and makes out the
news the thought crosses one's mind that the slate is wiped clean.
The sky is less grey than usual (see pp.65-6 below).

When Jaguar next appears in the Epilogue it is to reveal the
good side of his nature and to sow doubt as to whether he ever
was evil enough to have committed the crime at all. Finally,
Vargas Llosa, questioned on the matter, has declared himself
uncertain about Jaguar's guilt (*19*, p.101-2). Perhaps, in the
end, deciding whether or not he committed murder is crucially
important only if one insists on interpreting the novel in absolute
terms. Vargas Llosa's own view of criticisms of his vagueness
about Jaguar's guilt is that such criticisms are quite misplaced.
They derive from the wish to have absolute truth; it is true that
the novelist may try to 'totalize' the picture of reality, but it is
part of that reality to be ambiguous.

A number of problems confront the reader at the end, when
assessing Jaguar's character. The image of Jaguar created in the
academy is antipathetic. The authenticity of that image is
bolstered by the fact that it is an apparently objective one:
Jaguar's behaviour is observed from the outside, not simply by
the narrator but by a variety of other parties:

> Hay un personaje que representa, diría yo, el mundo
> objetivo, que es la pura objetividad, que está visto siempre
> desde fuera. (*14*, p.79)

In one way or another Jaguar is portrayed by means of third-person narrative, he does not argue his own case directly (compare the subjective portrayal of Boa). All this lends credence to the common image of a violent and insensitive personality. On the other hand, the reader is asked to reconcile this image with another one which is totally opposed to the first, presented in a subjective way and yet apparently nearer the truth. The reconciliation is conceptually difficult because by the time he is asked to make it the reader is so committed to the evil image of Jaguar. It is also structurally difficult in that the reader also realises at the same time how far Vargas Llosa has been playing with his sensibilities by deliberately withholding the evidence upon which an integral assessment of Jaguar could be made. It is this that has caused some critics to part company with the author and allude to perverseness on his part. Undeniably, the reader is faced with a trying discovery; I have already said that the novel is written to be re-read.

The question remains, was it necessary to keep the two sides of Jaguar—sensitive, loving, unfortunate on the one hand, *macho*, cruel, physically assertive on the other—so totally separate? Sharon Magnarelli argues persuasively that it was: hiding the identity of the *yo* allows for the convincing portrayal of the dualism of his character:

> A great deal of the novel's force results from the discovery that this *I*, with which we have been sympathising throughout, is Jaguar, the same third person we have been despising throughout. Had we known all along that the *I* was Jaguar, we would either see him as entirely different and feel that the other boys were unjust, or else we would perceive the *I* differently. It is only through this completely divided presentation and through our ignorance of the identity of the *I* that we are able to see Jaguar both ways and simultaneously accept the reliability of the *I* and recognise our own susceptibility to the powers of language. In addition, the final identification of the first person destroys the myth which has been built up. (*26*, p.43)

It is the Epilogue—which some have argued, quite mistakenly

in my view, is superfluous, which is

... society.

He leaves the centre of the stage of the Leoncio Prado theatre to merge into the ranks of the nondescript man in the street—or city—outside. The mythical hero becomes a bank clerk.

Jaguar's name is a small puzzle in itself. Like him, Boa has only a nickname but, unlike him, has only a college life. El Poeta is a nickname which can be shed when Alberto steps outside the college, and similarly Esclavo can become Ricardo Arana. Why then does Jaguar, who lives so fully outside the college, before and after, have no real name? Possibly Vargas Llosa is hinting that something of the aggressive self remains in his extra-collegiate existence. Without realising it, Teresa seems to suggest something similar near the very end by making as if to attack Jaguar; though not without a hint that affection can triumph over violence.

—Eres un vengativo—dijo Teresa.

Además, simuló golpearlo. Pero bajó la mano que había levantado burlonamente, la conservó en el aire mientras sus ojos, de improviso locuaces, lo desafiaban con dichosa insolencia. El Jaguar cogió la mano que lo amenazaba. Teresa se dejó ir contra él, apoyó el rostro en su pecho y, con la mano libre, lo abrazó. (p.340)

Before turning to broader questions of interpretation we must consider Gamboa, the last remaining principal character. The author regards him as a man who has never yet seen the system of which he is part put to the test. Hitherto everything has been unequivocally clear for him. His blind faith in the system, which he has never had reason to analyse, is shaken by the revelation of a new dimension to that system. It puts him in a great moral dilemma: 'Justamente para ser coherente y consecuente necesita violarlo [el sistema], perjudicarse él mismo. No se rebela. Acepta' (*4*, p.431). Almost every commentator has described Gamboa as a model soldier. Similarly, almost everyone sees him as a failure: 'Lo pierde todo, inclusive la fe en la vida militar, su vida' (*6*, p.119). The fact that Gamboa knows the regulations by heart is a measure of his dedication. That dedication is one factor that commands the respect of the cadets, who recognise that his harshness stems from commitment to the system and at the same time expect justice from him; it is to him that they turn when they wish to approach the authorities. Physically too, he commands respect (pp.150-1).

Following the death of Esclavo, Gamboa makes a report to the authorities, who conclude that he has lost his senses; the college cannot afford a scandal—'algo anda mal en su cabeza, Gamboa' (p.275). In the midst of Gamboa's uncertainties about whether and in what manner the investigation should proceed he receives a letter from his wife, who is expecting their child and missing him. When Alberto has been interviewed and threatened with the revelation of his pornographic writings, Gamboa is told to delete his report from the record; he accepts it as his military duty to do as he is told, even though this may not be in accordance with either the regulations or his own moral sense. On the question of his adherence to the regulations, his Captain observes:

Usted tiene un empacho de reglamentos...No lo critico, Gamboa, pero en la vida hay que ser práctico. (p.296)

Rules are to be interpreted; soldiers must be realists and take circumstances into account. What, then, is the point of Gamboa being stubborn and prejudicing his own position for one of the cadets? To pursue the matter of Alberto's denunciation can only create problems and the colonel is already angered by what has transpired so far. But Gamboa is unimpressed:

—Bah—dijo Gamboa, con desgano—¿Qué pueden hacerme? Además, me importa muy poco. Tengo la conciencia limpia.

—Con la conciencia tranquila se gana el cielo—dijo el

capitán, pero no siempre los colores (...206)

collapses just as his daughter is being born.

Gamboa is true to his own standards, which present him with an impossible choice. Should he heed his moral duty by pursuing the investigation of the presumed murder, or should he abide by the dictates of his superiors, in accordance with his military duty? Insofar as he tries to live up to his own precepts he is like Jaguar, however different they may seem in externals. Each has a certain moral dignity—which Alberto rather lacks—but the reward in each case is obscurity: Gamboa is posted to the hills ('Voy a ver muchas vicunãs...Y a lo mejor aprenderé quechua'; p.322), Jaguar merges into the ranks of minor bureaucrats.

Since Alberto is also a moral failure, the fate of these main characters supports Luchting's view that failure is one of Vargas Llosa's main themes (*32*). The military education fails—in an absolute sense, because it is not true education, and in a practical sense because it does not instil its own standards in the boys. Gamboa fails because he is wholly dedicated to an ideal concept of the military machine:

> Gamboa fracasa precisamente porque intenta la realización de lo que la educación castrense pretende ser, educación que está basada en la frustración entelequial desde un principio. (*8*, p.232)

But even Luchting accepts that there are relative successes too, compromises within the limits of the *status quo*. The colonel is a minor character who illustrates this line of thought perfectly. Or consider Alberto, quick to get the measure of his society and use his intelligence to play the system. Even Jaguar can be thought of as successfully adapted to that system of bourgeois values.[11] In all cases it is the system that wins, not the individual. Is it therefore right to conclude that the military education is wholly irrelevant to the outcome? Has it not taught, by representing society at large, that the individual is hemmed in by the social structure in which he lives, and that that structure has no real moral justification?

The argument that *La ciudad y los perros* is a moral novel has been most insistently advanced by Lafforgue. He claims, for example, that Jaguar is a figure of judgement who sees that there is neither honour nor solidarity in those around him, who recognises their corruption:

> ...todo está falseado en este mundo, este mundo es una enorme trampa, y quienes en él no recurren al engaño son harapos, larvas, détritus, miseria humana, unos cobardes sin otro fin que la muerte, como el Esclavo. (*29*, p.107)

Jaguar, having learned the dirty ways of the world, finally accepts that he must go along with it. The timid and innocuous child faced with a hostile world of violence and corruption has met that world on its own terms and been driven into submission. For Alberto, of course, the passage was calmer: he faced neither the economic nor the personal trials, was quick to recover from moral uncertainties and make a conscious choice to conform when it seemed opportune. Jaguar looks all the while for a positive or honourable act from those around him, something which might point to progress or hope for the future, but there seems to be none forthcoming either in or out of the college; perhaps, after all, he is too much of a romantic. Lafforgue contrasts the presentation of Jaguar with those of Alberto and Esclavo. The other cadets perceive Jaguar as an instrument of evil but the reader is to realise, throught the *yo* monologues, that 'no es mucho más que su acendrado amor a una tierna muchachita' (*29*, p.106). There is a striking similarity here with the softness of the child Richi.

In the course of a somewhat involved and wordy argument Lafforgue concludes that Jaguar was fundamentally good but

---

[11]Luchting (*32*) notes that some of the figures in *La casa verde*, the author's next novel, do, however, succeed outside the established system of values.

we accept that Jaguar is ultimately good this does not require us to conclude that goodness triumphs over an evil system.

Redeeming human qualities can be found in other characters too. The most obvious parallel to Jaguar is Gamboa, under whose rigid militarism there lies a devoted and tender family man, as revealed in his letters and photos, in the references to the family home. Three factors in particular converge at the end of the book to suggest that Gamboa is abandoning assertive maleness in favour of more submissive qualities: his mention of the vicuña (quoted above), its habitat the *puna* region to which Gamboa is destined, and the birth of his child, significantly a daughter. The school vicuña is used for target practice by the cadets, throwing stones in the parade-ground. Gamboa is not quite a martyr, but he does not have the material compensations afforded to the other failures. Such modest compensations as he does have are somewhat like those of Jaguar, it is true, but more exclusively in the area of human love: what might have been a distinguished career comes to nothing.[12]

The vicuña is discovered, without explanation, wandering in the Leoncio Prado parade-ground. Its proper place is the Andes, an observation suitably made by that other *serrano*, Cava. 'Se parece a los indios', he reflects (p.13), perhaps unconscious of the fact that to the other cadets he is one himself: it is Boa who comments on Cava's Indian features. Cava, of course, is banished back to the sierra where he belongs, another victim of the action. Voicing the principle that each will find his designated place in the social order, the author has Flaco

[12]Militarism receives special attention in *27* and *33*.

Higueras close the novel with the words 'la cabra tira al monte' (p.343).

Animal imagery is very pervasive, extending far beyond the obvious nicknames. The *perros* are adolescent pups, inclined to animal behaviour, learning to survive in a dog-eat-dog society. Esclavo might be thought of as the runt of the pack. The name *perro* also acquires a pejorative value, both because of its scornful use by cadets in other years and by association with general usages like 'vida perra' and 'hijo de perra'. (I have already mentioned the author's short novel *Los cachorros*; in *Pantaleón y las visitadoras* the protagonist dreams of soldiers transformed into dogs.) The Darwinian struggle in which the boys become involved gives the lie to the Captain's declaration: 'Métanse en la mollera que están en las Fuerzas Armadas y no en un zoológico' (p.240). Peruvian society, as represented by the school, is a jungle in which animals fight to survive. Officials also behave like dogs (p.261); Esclavo is made to act out the role at his initiation (p.49), barking and foaming like a rabid dog. The reference to 'huevos de acero' (p.23), essential in order to survive in the society of the cadets, neatly demonstrates the *machismo* of that society and calls to mind the case of Pichula Cuéllar,[13] castrated by a mad dog. Normal behaviour for the cadets involves the transgression of natural human standards and approximates to that of the animal world. Once the drama is over:

> En las clases, los cadetes hablaban, se insultaban, se escupían, se bombardeaban con proyectiles de papel, insultaban a los profesores imitando relinchos, bufidos, fruñidos, maullidos, ladridos: la vida era otra vez normal. (p.316)

Other animal imagery is used for caricature: the Colonel walks like a seagull (p.224), the Captain lies ready to pounce like a piranha (p.254), Pitaluga buries his head like a tortoise (p.154). Teresa's unattractive aunt has a hand like a mollusc and bends over like a 'gran mamífero' (p.86). Military events are

[13]'Pichula' is slang for penis.

madres y esposas son figuras opacas, desvaídas, resignadas ante
el atropello viril' (*39*, p.36).

Women in general come off badly in Vargas Llosa's novels:
they are rarely characterized in any depth and often serve as
sexual toys. Vargas Llosa seems almost to replace the
reassurance of the mother figure with the image of the brothel as
refuge. The love of Jaguar for Teresa and of Gamboa for his
wife stands out against a background of sexual perversion and
superficial relationships.

In general this novel demythologises, and one of the myths it
exposes is that of romantic love in an ideal adult world. Myths
are created in the cadet society, built on sexual fantasies (Pies
Dorados) or the powers of alcohol, both related to manhood.
The inconsequentiality, the emptiness of the greatest myth, that
of Jaguar, is one of the novel's principal statements, although
we should remember that it has long been the case that the
protagonist of the modern novel is anti-hero as much as hero.

Vargas Llosa is not above making Nature conform to the
moods of his characters or reflect the development of the action.
For example, just before the manoeuvres in which Esclavo is
shot, Gamboa awakens to an overcast sky (p.153). At the end of
the novel, when he learns the news of his daughter's birth and
leaves the academy for good, he looks out to sea, and again:

...estaba menos gris que de costumbre; las olas reventaban
en la orilla y morían casi instantáneamente. (p.326)

The reference to grey is particularly important; Vargas Llosa
makes use of the fact that for much of the year Lima is
enveloped in its *garúa*, a fine wet mist. In his fiction he makes
the sun shine rarely, clears the sky at moments of significant

advance in the story. The college is usually in a mist, its images are often described as hazy, the light as muted. Vargas Llosa uses increases in light as if he were operating a spotlight, to emphasize a dramatic action by its starkness. Oviedo (*6*) was the first to note this and relate it to changes in style; his observations are carried further by Hancock (*42*), especially in his comments on the closing description of the Leoncio Prado (p.317), in which he argues that contrasts of light and darkness have a connotative value. Perhaps the most engaging use of light is to develop personality, as is the case, for instance, when Teresa, calculating possibilities in a way which suggests she is less naive than one might suppose, has her eyes lit by a 'luz maliciosa' (p.138). Tusa (*31*) gives more examples illustrating contrasts of light/heat and darkness/cold.

The Leoncio Prado is a microcosm of Peruvian society in which are represented its ethnic stands (Cava, Vallano) and its social divisions (Jaguar, Esclavo, Alberto, the *serranos* and costeños); it is governed by a military regime which is authoritarian and corrupt. (Peru was under the military government of Odría from 1948 to 1956, and has intermittently been under military rule since.) There is no doubt that Vargas Llosa, marked to the core by his own experiences in the school, has tried faithfully to evoke the way it reflected the different strata of Peruvian society. The events he describes are imaginary—it seems no-one was murdered—but faithful in spirit to the life the boys led; minor details confirm this—the French teacher Fontana, for example, apparently based on the poet and teacher César Moro. All Vargas Llosa's novels are imaginative elaborations of very specific experiences in his own life in Peru. There is also no doubt that he is deeply concerned with the injustices of that society. To quote Carlos Fuentes:

> La novela...*La ciudad y los perros* cala como ninguna otra este sentido de la justicia en América Latina: esta radical ausencia de inocencia en la sociedad, esta imposibilidad de inocencia. (*8*, p.53)

Vargas Llosa paints a raw picture of that society, hiding no shortcomings and pulling no punches on the matter of its power

people conform. Do all the

signs of both resistance and hope. To paraphrase Sartre, even

the characters' attempts to make something of themselves given
their situation do come to grief, some redeeming human
qualities are evinced in the process. There is, in Jaguar and
Gamboa, some good that survived.

Oviedo (*6*, p.106) is right to take issue with Boldori and Harss
(*4*, pp.422, 425, 433) over the question of determinism on the
grounds that it is a causal over-simplification: he chooses instead
to speak of fatalism, being a term which better allows for 'la
oscura ramificación de los móviles humanos'. Fate certainly
plays a rôle: the game of chance which opens the action points to
this. Whether fatalism is a substantially better term or not, what
is clear is that Vargas Llosa, following Sartre, leaves his
characters the freedom to act and affect their destinies. That
freedom is strictly circumscribed by their current situation. As if
by way of exemplification, Gamboa (p.40) tells the cadets that
'son libres de elegir', the choice being between a kick in the arse
or loss of good conduct marks. But it is still a degree of freedom.

Vargas Llosa's characters are not simply the products of an
overwhelming social and economic environment, they are free
agents within the limits of their circumstances; they are
constantly faced with options and are thus responsible for their
own destinies. To some extent the form of narration reflects this
uneasy marriage of social determinism and existentialism:
characters are not analysed only through the medium of an
omniscient author, they also appear to assert their personalities
in several more subjective and direct appeals to the reader.

At the end of *La ciudad y los perros* Vargas Llosa does not

abandon hope altogether; however, his view of the social system
is wholly negative and on balance his view of human nature is
pessimistic. Faced with the exigencies of academy life the boys
act rôles in order to mask their insecurities and doubts.
Adolescence and the passage to adult standards and responsi-
bilities is a traumatic experience: the epigraph to part two, taken
from Paul Nizan, says as much:

> J'avais vingt ans. Je ne laisserai personne dire que c'est le
> plus bel âge de la vie.[14]

But the most conclusive quotation used by the author is the one
which introduces the Epilogue. It comes from a poem by Carlos
Germán Belli:

> ...en cada linaje el deterioro ejerce su dominio.

The pessimism underlying this statement is ineluctable, although
one may wonder still whether the decadence of which it speaks is
inherent in human nature or whether it is the product of external
social pressures. Obviously Vargas Llosa envisages no progress
(*34*, p.17); the undermining of linear progression in the narrative
reflects this in a formal way.

Violence is not simply a characteristic of the adolescent world:
it is something which pervades society and is endemic in Latin
America. The author's attitude to life has almost a Jesuit
flavour; it also recalls the biblical 'Militia est vita hominis super
terram'.[15]

> ...la misma vida en sociedad impone al hombre una serie
> de pruebas constantes, de pugnas permanentes...Yo creo
> que en un país como el mío la violencia está en la base de
> todas las relaciones humanas...El individuo se afirma, se
> consolida socialmente venciendo resistencias de toda
> índole. La personalidad se forma imponiéndose a los
> otros. (*4*, p.432)

For all this, Vargas Llosa has declared himself surprised that he
should be thought a pessimist: the triumph of a personal ethic

---

[14]'I was twenty. No-one is going to tell me that that is the happiest time of your
life.'

[15]'Man's life on earth is a struggle.' From the (Vulgate) Bible: Job, vii.1.

is possible (*19*, p.101).

4. Conclusion

While there can be no doubt about Vargas Llosa's disaffection with the Peruvian establishment, there is equally no doubt that his guiding principles are literary rather than ideological. Apart from his own declarations to that effect (see pp.13-15 above) there is ample evidence of a literary intent in the text of *La ciudad y los perros*.

The established institutions—the military, the church (see pp. 103-4), the political machine (nationally and internationally, the latter being evoked in the person of the U.S. lady ambassador)—conspire to maintain solidarity and reduce doubt or dissent (cf *39*, p. 139). Vargas Llosa's fiction, on the other hand, sows doubt; instead of simply advocating a different social order, or even the demise of the existing one, his statements about society in *La ciudad y los perros* are a little ambiguous. The very structure of the text postulates that appearances are deceptive, that language should not be trusted, that reality is complex. Because reality is complex, then complex means are necessary to capture it (*37*, p. 276).

Most notable modern Latin-American writers have had to resist demands that they write explicit propaganda. In Vargas Llosa's case the degree of commitment to criticism of the *status quo* is not in question, but the manner of his writing results from literary considerations. The difficulty of the text, its changes of style and perspective, its disruption of linear narrative, all lead to an obfuscation of the issues, and require perseverance from the reader. In *Pantaleón y las visitadoras* (which is, however, complex in a more covert way) Vargas Llosa returns to the military as a kind of metaphor for a bureaucratic and self-satisfied society (see *35*, p. 61). This time he debunks the institution more simply by means of high farce, when captain Pantaleón Pantoja is put in charge of the prostitutes who are [illegible] would argue, is such [illegible] straightforward and unequivocal attack on the system. All the same, the novel as it stands remains a powerful indictment:

> Un verdadero proceso al Colegio Militar y a las formas de la institucionalidad peruana. No es una crítica procaz, sino una mostración descarnada; no una censura gruesa, sino un precisar la pauperización del contenido moral de ciertos núcleos humanos, lo que es absolutamente válido para toda Hispanoamérica. (*3*, p. 421)

The different perspectives serve to enrich the action since they give different views of an essentially limited set of phenomena; they constitute a formal realisation of what the author referred to as the tremendous relativity of human experience (*19*, p. 103). Rarely, if ever, is any one individual in possession of a complete or absolute picture of events: truth consists of a sum of perspectives which are not necessarily even simultaneous. 'No hay una verdad, apenas verdades contingentes, perspectivas cambiantes' (*8*, p. 157). Sartre claims that:

> ...notre problème technique est de trouver une orchestration des consciences qui nous permette de rendre la pluridimensionalité de l'évènement. De plus, en renonçant à la fiction du narrateur tout-connaissant, nous avons assumé l'obligation de supprimer les intermédiaires entre le lecteur et les subjectivités-points de vue de nos personnages; il s'agit de le faire entrer dans les consciences comme dans un moulin, il faut même qu'il coïncide successivement avec chacune d'entre elles.[16]

[16] 'Our technical problem is to achieve an orchestration of consciousnesses which will allow us to convey the multi-dimensionality of events. Furthermore, in rejecting the fiction of a narrator who knows all we assume the responsibility

Sartre's last words here recall those of Vargas Llosa about every technique being designed to eliminate the distance between the reader and the action (see above, p. 20). The sudden initial immersion of the reader in the action, with no descriptive preliminaries, is part of that design, and quite obviously the aim thereafter is to make the reader experience, in turn, the full intensity of different characters' perceptions and sensibilities. It is doubtful, however, whether the closeness is always maintained. How is it possible for the reader to experience the events viscerally and yet so frequently be faced with a new narrative mode? The constant changes of pace, style and narrator militate against that closeness because the reader is never left for long to forget the need to readjust to another change. Although the author is subtle enough when he is third-person narrator, and in any case not a dominant voice, one is aware of him operating at another remove as the constructor of the overall narrative design. Vargas Llosa is not wholly successful, then, in his aim to tell a story in which the reader will believe and become completely involved; as he acknowledges himself: 'si el lector divisa al autor interviniendo, actuando vicariamente, agazapado detrás de los personajes, la ficción se derrumba...' (*15*, p. 23). Nor is Vargas Llosa as impartial as he pretends to be (*39*, p. 28; *20*, p. 38).

For the reader to be made to work is nothing out of the ordinary in modern fiction, but it is a phenomenon which usually undermines verisimilitude. To the extent that conscious narrative machinations and the desire for a believable fictional reality are incompatible here they produce a tension which, I believe, underlies the criticisms of a number of commentators. Harss, for example, talks of the author's 'mala costumbre...de querer intrigar al lector'. Having referred to the hiding of Jaguar's *yo*, he complains that its eventual revelation 'sólo ofusca y distrae. Es que Vargas Llosa nos despista injustamente,

of doing away with any intermediaries between the reader and the subjectivities/points of view of our characters; it is a matter of drawing him into their consciousness as if he were being thrown into a mill; he must even be made to coincide with each of them in turn.' *Qu'est-ce que la littérature?* (Paris: Gallimard, 1948), p. 371.

ˈ ⸍⸍ ⸗ ⸗⸗⸅ The

three fold relationship

believable and at the same time it is apparent that she is a fictional artifice. Here, perhaps, is the feature which best illustrates the paradox of Vargas Llosa. He writes to tell a story and make the reader believe in it—an illusive enterprise of a very traditional kind, and a refreshing one in the context of modern fictional trends. Yet he tries to achieve this by palpably artificial means.

One area in which the reader's belief is not severely tested is the borderline between reality and fantasy, an area favoured by so many contemporary Latin-American writers. This is presumably what Antonio Skármeta is referring to when he writes of Vargas Llosa's 'inmunidad al delirio' (*36*, p. 204). Just as there is no humour, there is little psychology, no metaphysics.[17] Vargas Llosa starts and ends with his feet firmly on the ground. Harss (*40*, p. 499) talks of Vargas Llosa 'shuffling the bits of the puzzle to heighten their effect, not...reordering perception'. There are no real flights of fancy of the kind one finds in García Márquez or Cortázar, for instance. There are, of course, adolescent fantasies in *La ciudad y los perros*, but the reader is asked to believe that they are only that, fantasies in the minds of young boys, and that the other dimension of reality is impervious to them.

La ciudad y los perros follows in a substantial tradition of novels about schools and adolescence: Golding's *Lord of the Flies*, Musil's *Törless*, Sartre's *L'Enfance d'un chef*, Salinger's *Catcher in the Rye* or, to take a more obscure but geographically

[17]Vargas Llosa once declared himself totally immune to humour in literature (*4*, p. 445). However, in his two most recent novels he appears to have caught the disease himself.

closer example, the Brazilian Raul Pompeia's *O Atheneu*. The
most illustrative comparison, however, can probably be made
with Lindsay Anderson's *If...*, a film of life in an English public
school. Similar struggles for self-discovery take place in an
authoritarian environment bolstered by the cadet force and the
chaplaincy. Similar myths, rituals, distasteful and abusive
behaviour apply amongst those boys. Trips into the
neighbouring town represent freedom, and into those trips are
fed sequences of rebellious and sexual fantasy, filmed in black
and white to contrast with the colour used otherwise. The film
concludes with a pitched battle between the boys and the forces
of the establishment. The crucial difference is that in *If...* the
fantasies have spilled over into reality and in that way it can
suggest that change is possible.

That this one novel should have attracted so much attention
from critics is a measure of its interest. By the author's own
criteria *La ciudad y los perros* is not wholly successful as a novel.
It escapes crude documentary realism and fully vindicates the
author's literary vocation, but it does not quite live up to his
ideal of autonomy, with the author out of the picture. While
some have complained of confusion and ambiguity, others have
held the latter a strength and recognised the artistic intention
behind the former. For these reasons, and for .its periodic
intensity of feeling, *La ciudad y los perros* is a provocative
novel. Not least among its interesting features is its difference
from other contemporary works of Latin America, a difference
typical of Vargas Llosa's work in general. Unanimously, *La
ciudad y los perros* has been held to raise Peruvian fiction onto a
new level. And looking to Latin America at large, when so many
authors seem to be indulging in experimentation for its own
sake, it is reassuring to find that Vargas Llosa has not lost sight
of the fact that writing a good novel means, amongst other
things, telling a good story.

Critical Studies

Texas Studies in Language and Literature, XIX, 4 (Winter 1977), and *World Literature Today*, LII, 1 (Winter 1978), are special issues on Vargas Llosa. A number of articles from them are listed below, under their authors' names, with the abbreviations *Texas Studies* (1977) and *World Literature* (1978).

1. Rilda L. Baker, 'Of how to be and what to see while you are being: The Reader's Performance in *The Time of the Hero*', *Texas Studies* (1977), 396-407.

2. Gordon Brotherston, *The Emergence of the Latin American Novel* (Cambridge: U.P., 1977). Discussions of several writers based on the analysis of selected extracts; one essay is on Vargas Llosa.

3. Raúl Silva Cáceres: review of the novel in *Cuadernos Hispanoamericanos*, 173 (May, 1964), 416-22. One of the best early reviews.

4. Luis Harss, *Los nuestros* (Buenos Aires: Editorial Sudamericana, 1966). Based on taperecorded interviews, this is rather journalistic but still contains many enlightening statements by Vargas Llosa.

5. Gerald Martin, 'Vargas Llosa: nueva novela y realismo', *Norte*, XII, 5-6 (1971), 112-21. Interesting but general study. Considers the author as a fundamentally conservative writer. Emphasizes his difference from contemporaries.

6. José Miguel Oviedo, *Mario Vargas Llosa: la invención de una realidad*, 2nd edition (Barcelona: Barral, 1977). Much the most thorough and accessible book on Vargas Llosa.

7. Elena Poniatowska, 'Al fin, un escritor que le apasiona escribir...', in the supplement 'La cultura en México' to the magazine *Siempre* (Mexico City), 117 (7 July 1965).

8. Helmy F. Giacoman and José Miguel Oviedo, *Homenaje a Mario Vargas Llosa* (New York: Las Américas, 1971). A collection of reprinted articles, of which the most interesting are listed separately in this Bibliographical Note. See also *29* and *36*.

9. Emir Rodríguez Monegal, 'Madurez de Vargas Llosa', *Mundo Nuevo*, 3 (September, 1966), 62-72. Also in *8*, *29* and *36*.

10. Mario Vargas Llosa, 'El papel del intelectual en los movimientos de liberación nacional', *Casa de las Américas*, VI, 35 (1966), 97-8.

11. Mario Vargas Llosa, 'Social Commitment and the Latin American Writer', *World Literature Today* (1978), 6-14.

12. Mario Vargas Llosa, *La orgía perpetua: Flaubert y Mme Bovary* (Barcelona: Seix Barral, 1975). One of the author's two major critical studies.

13. Mario Vargas Llosa, *García Márquez: historia de un deicidio* (Barcelona: Barral, 1971).

14. Luis Agüero, Juan Larco and Ambrosio Fornet, 'Sobre *La ciudad y los perros*, de Mario Vargas Llosa', *Casa de las Américas*, V, 30 (May-June, 1965), 63-80. Round-table discussion including the author.

15. Mario Vargas Llosa, 'Carta de batalla por *Tirant lo Blanc*', prologue to the edition by Alianza Editorial (Madrid, 1969).

16. Mario Vargas Llosa, *La novela*. The text of a lecture given in a place which is identified only as Universidad de la República on 11 August 1966 and published in the series Cuadernos de Literatura/2, Fundación de Cultura Universitaria. Oviedo, in his bibliography to *6*, gives the place of publication as Montevideo.

17. Mario Vargas Llosa, 'En torno a la nueva novela en Latinoamérica', in Germán Gullón and Agnes Gullón (eds), *Teoría de la novela* (Madrid: Taurus, 1974).

18. Oscar Collazos, Julio Cortázar and Mario Vargas Llosa, *Literatura en la revolución y revolución en la literatura* (Mexico City: Siglo XXI Editores, 1970).

19. R. Cano Gaviría, *El buitre y el ave fénix: Conversaciones con Mario Vargas Llosa* (Barcelona: Anagrama, 1972). Very interesting discussion with author, followed by a less useful essay.

Texas Studies (1977), 514-21.

24. Carlos Fuentes, 'El afán totalizante de Vargas Llosa', in *8*, pp. 24-30.

25. Alexander Coleman, 'The Transfiguration of the Chivalric Novel', in *World Literature* (1978), 24-30.

26. Sharon Magnarelli, '*The Time of the Hero*: Liberty Enslaved', *Latin American Literary Review*, IV, 8 (1976), 35-45. Interesting on language but not helped by constant critical name-dropping.

27. Joseph Sommers, 'Literatura e ideología: la evolución novelística del militarismo en Vargas Llosa', *Hispamérica*, IV, 1 (1975), 83-117. Mostly concerned with social aspects.

28. Georg Rudolf Lind, 'Mario Vargas Llosa y el atropello de los indefensos', *Humboldt*, 54 (1974), 62-7. Defends the author against his critics and supports Lafforgue's interpretation.

29. Jorge Lafforgue, 'La ciudad y los perros, novela moral', in María Rosa Alonso *et al.*, *Agresión a la realidad: Mario Vargas Llosa*, Inventarios Provisionales (Las Palmas: 1971), pp. 79-125. This volume is a collection of reprints which overlaps considerably with *8* and *36*.

30. Rosa Boldori, *Mario Vargas Llosa y la literatura en el Perú de hoy* (Santa Fe, Argentina: Ediciones Colmegna, 1969). The 'determinismo ambiental' interpretation.

31. Bobs M. Tusa, 'Mario Vargas Llosa: The Profane Optimist', *Hispanófila*, 59 (January, 1977), 75-88 and 60 (May, 1977), 59-76. The first part of this article deals mainly with oriental philosophy. The second part interprets Vargas Llosa in the light of the first. While the observations on his novels are interesting, it is doubtful whether the preamble is a necessary means of arriving at them and there seems to be nothing in Vargas Llosa's biography to suggest that an oriental approach is specially apt.

32.   Wolfgang Luchting, 'Los fracasos de Mario Vargas Llosa', in *Agresión a la realidad* (see *29*), pp. 141-78. An almost identical article by him appears in *8* under a similar title.

33.   Casto Manuel Fernández, *Aproximación formal a la novelística de Vargas Llosa* (Madrid: Editora Nacional, 1977). Formal, as the title suggests. Good on Gamboa and the hierarchy of power.

34.   Ariel Dorfman, 'Mario Vargas Llosa y José María Arguedas: dos visiones de una sola América', in *Imaginación y violencia en América* (Santiago de Chile: Editorial Universitaria, 1970), pp. 193-223. Reprinted in *8*.

35.   Elena Poniatowska *et al.* (eds), *Antología mínima de Mario Vargas Llosa* (Buenos Aires: Tiempo Contemporáneo, 1969).

36.   Luis Alfonso Díez (ed.), *Asedios a Vargas Llosa* (Santiago de Chile: Editorial Universitaria, 1972). A collection of reprinted articles, many of which also appear in *8* and in *Agresión a la realidad* (see *29*).

37.   Frank Dauster, 'Aristotle and Vargas Llosa: Literature, History and the Interpretation of Reality', *Hispania* (U.S.A.), LIII (1970), 273-7.

38.   José Escobar, 'Mario Vargas Llosa: *La ciudad y los perros*', *Revista de Occidente*, IX, 26 (May, 1965), 261-7. A good early review.

39.   Rosa Boldori de Baldussi, *Vargas Llosa: un narrador y sus demonios* (Buenos Aires: Fernando García Cambeiro, 1974). A structuralist study and rather given to jargon. Interesting on myth and on narrative organisation. Attempts to counter Oviedo's criticism of the deterministic view she expressed earlier in *30*.

40.   Luis Harss, 'A City Boy', in *Texas Studies* (1977), 495-502. More journalese but not without interest.

41.   George R. McMurray, 'Form and Content Relationships in Vargas Llosa's *La ciudad y los perros*', *Hispania* (U.S.A.), LVI (1973), 579-86. More useful than his 'The Novels of Mario Vargas Llosa', *Modern Language Quarterly*, XXIX (1968), 329-40.

42.   Joel Hancock, 'Animalization and Chiaroscuro Techniques: Descriptive Language in *La ciudad y los perros*', *Latin American Literary Review*, IV, 7 (1975), 137-47. Limited in scope, but persuasive.

44.

1973). Chap

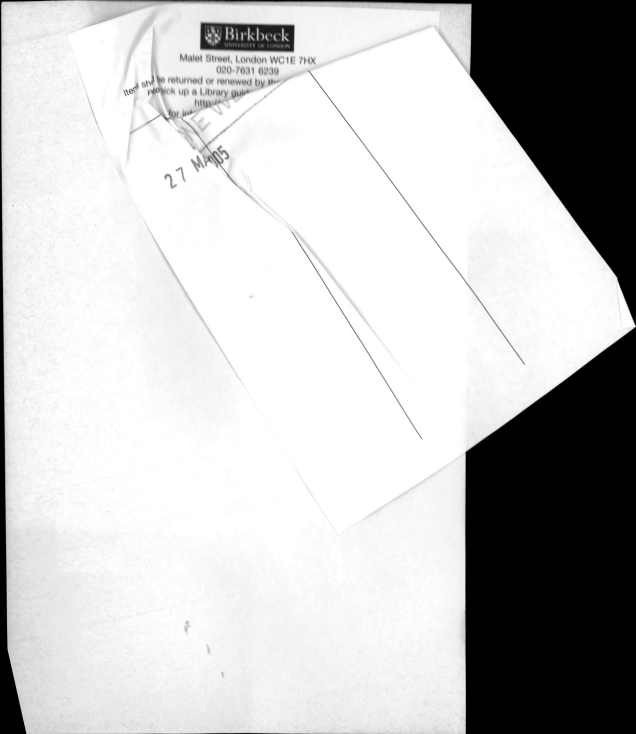

... in Cleethorpes public library. She also had a craze for all kinds of American literature, especially detective stories, and went on to study American literature at Warwick University. Then she became a teacher. She taught in Malawi, Africa (she still has a scar on her ankle from a mosquito bite that went septic), and in County Durham, England. She has three *adorable* teenage children (she has to say that – they might read this book!): Laura, Alex and Chris.

Previously published as *Sea Hags, Suckers and Cobra Sharks*

Other books by Susan Gates

KILLER MUSHROOMS ATE MY GRAN
REVENGE OF THE TOFFEE MONSTER

of the Tentacled Terror

PUFFIN BOOKS

PUFFIN BOOKS

Published by the Penguin Group
Penguin Books Ltd, 80 Strand, London WC2R 0RL, England
Penguin Putnam Inc., 375 Hudson Street, New York, New York 10014, USA
Penguin Books Australia Ltd, Ringwood, Victoria, Australia
Penguin Books Canada Ltd, 10 Alcorn Avenue, Toronto, Ontario, Canada M4V 3B2
Penguin Books India (P) Ltd, 11 Community Centre, Panchsheel Park, New Delhi – 110 017, India
Penguin Books (NZ) Ltd, Cnr Rosedale and Airborne Roads, Albany, Auckland, New Zealand
Penguin Books (South Africa) (Pty) Ltd, 24 Sturdee Avenue, Rosebank 2196 South Africa

Penguin Books Ltd, Registered Offices: 80 Strand, London WC2R 0RL, England

www.penguin.com

First published as *Sea Hags, Suckers and Cobra Sharks* by Puffin Books 1998
This edition published in Puffin Books 2000
2

Copyright © Susan Gates, 1998
All rights reserved

The moral right of the author has been asserted

Filmset in Monotype Baskerville

Made and printed in England by Clays Ltd, St Ives plc

British Library Cataloguing in Publication Data
A CIP catalogue record for this book is available from the British Library

ISBN 0-141-30672-6

'This is an emergency!' said Mum, checking her diary. 'The school holidays are only a week away. What are we going to do with George?'

I was busy zapping little green aliens on the computer screen. But I turned down their screams so I could hear what Mum and Dad were saying.

'Well, I can't look after him,' said Dad. 'I've got very important business in Brussels.'

'Well, I can't,' said Mum. 'I've got a conference in Cardiff.'

'Can't you take him with you?'

'Impossible! Why can't you take him with you?'

'Impossible!'

'I could always stay here,' I suggested. 'Like that kid in *Home Alone*.'

'Impossible!' they both shouted.

Whoosh, whoosh! I fired my flamethrower and a couple of aliens melted.

Dad put down his *Business News*. 'So what *are* we going to do with George?' he asked Mum.

'I am here, you know. I do *exist*!'

But no one was listening to me.

I twitched my specs further up my nose, then changed to the evil villain and wiped out a couple of earthlings. *Zap, zap!* Die, you puny earthling scum.

'Everyone's let us down,' said Mum, flicking through her address book. 'Mrs Perkins is getting a new hip. Just when we need her! There's absolutely no one to take George off our hands for the half-term holidays.'

Then Mum's finger stopped halfway down the page.

'What about your Aunt Primrose?' she asked Dad.

'Who? said Dad, looking even more puzzled than usual.

... who's lived for ... the ...

'Who is Aun... nobody bothered to answer.

Mum shoved the phone at Dad. 'You ring her up. She's *your* aunt.'

Dad backed away. 'She's my *great*-aunt, actually, though I usually just call her Aunt. But is this a good idea? I haven't seen her for ages. We never had much to do with that side of the family. We thought they were – well, very strange.'

'All right, *you* suggest someone to look after George!' said Mum in her dangerous voice.

Dad took the phone. 'Seems a bit of a cheek,' he muttered feebly, 'to ring her up after all this time.'

'Never mind that,' said Mum. 'This is a crisis situation. Besides, she stayed here once. You remember, for one night, years ago. When she came on a shopping trip to

London. So she owes us a favour, doesn't she?'

'I'd forgotten that,' said Dad. And, with Mum's address book in one hand, he began punching in the numbers.

I swivelled round in my chair.

I started to say, 'But I don't know any Great-Aunt Primrose –'

'*Shhh, shhh,*' said Mum, waving me to be quiet. She wanted to hear what Dad was saying.

'Great!' Dad was saying. 'That's really good of you. That's saved our lives. Yes, yes, yes, yes. See you Sunday.'

Dad put down the phone. He was smiling. 'She'll take him,' he said. 'We can drop him off there on Sunday. Crisis over. I don't know what all the fuss was about.'

He picked up his paper again.

A sort of doubtful expression was mixing with the relief on Mum's face.

'What did she sound like over the phone?' she asked Dad. 'I mean, she must be nearly seventy. Did she sound senile or anything? I don't want to leave Georgie with just *anyone.*'

4

'She sounded sharp as a razor,' said

PRIMROSE.

'Yes, you do, George,' said Mum. Her voice was all brisk and businesslike, as if she was warning me not to make a fuss. 'She stayed here once. Drab little person. Very ordinary. Plump, tweedy suit, white flyaway hair. You remember –'

'Of course he doesn't remember,' said Dad. 'He was only four at the time.'

He looked over his paper at me. 'Can't be helped, George, I'm afraid. It'll be a bit dull with old Auntie. But it's only a week. You can handle that, can't you? You're a cool customer. A grown-up sort of chap. And I'll bring you a big, big present back. What about that, eh?'

'It'd better be a very big one,' I told him.

I swivelled back to my game. There were

5

earthlings scuttling all over the place. *Zap, zap, zap!* I got every last one of them.

'I'm so pleased that's fixed up,' said Mum. She scribbled a note in her diary, then snapped it shut.

'Problem solved,' she said.

That very same day, I started remembering things about Great-Aunt Primrose. Things that had been locked up in my mind since I was four years old. At first, they were just scraps of things. Like eyes that were wise and kind. And hair that looked like white candyfloss.

Then more and more memories came crowding out.

'When she came to London for a shopping trip, did this Primrose person take any notice of me?' I asked Mum.

Mum shrugged. 'Well, she *did* stay ages in your bedroom. She seemed to prefer your company to ours.'

'She did notice me!' I suddenly remembered. 'She cuddled me in her arms.

We talked for ages and ages. And her arms felt all soft and cushiony.'

Then I remembered something else. Something that had happened late at night, that time she came to stay. I was supposed to be asleep. But I wanted to talk to her again. So I climbed out of bed and went looking for her.

Aunt Primrose was standing in front of her bedroom mirror. Her tweedy suit was folded up on a chair. And she was trying on a new swimming costume.

I remember thinking, 'Wow! Where did she buy that? That's the brightest swimming costume in the whole of London.'

It was brighter than a carnival costume. It was the most razzling-dazzling costume ever. It was golden like sunshine – with lime green stripes!

Aunt Primrose twirled and twirled in front of the mirror, admiring her new swimming costume.

Then an amazing thing happened. I couldn't believe it. I crouched in the shadows, goggle-eyed.

Because the pattern on the swimming

colour, like a green and gold fire.

Until the whole of Aunt Primrose was dancing with green and gold tiger stripes chasing each other like waves all over her body!

Then Mum called up the stairs. 'George, are you out of bed?'

And the pattern began shrinking back.

I remember thinking, 'Oh, that's really sad.' I wasn't scared or anything. I wanted to see some more. It was great. Like watching my own private firework display.

But when Mum shouted, 'I'm coming up there!' the fireworks stopped. The green and gold shrivelled back to the swimsuit where it belonged. And Aunt Primrose's legs and arms went back to normal. All pink and dimply, like before.

She knew I was hiding there. I'm sure

she did. She seemed to know, by radar or something. Because she winked at me in the mirror. As if she'd put on that show just for me. As if it was a secret between us.

'Come on,' I told myself. 'That couldn't have happened. You were only a little kid then. You probably dreamed it or something.'

'This Primrose person,' I checked with Mum. 'That time she came, when I was four years old, did you say she was *ordinary*?'

'Oh, quite ordinary,' said Mum, stuffing some papers into her briefcase. 'You wouldn't notice her in a crowd.'

'There you are,' I reassured myself. 'Quite ordinary. So you can't really have seen her changing colour. You must have imagined it.'

Then, the next day, I remembered something else.

'She asked me a riddle,' I told Mrs Perkins who came to look after me after school.

'Who did?'

'My Aunt Primrose. When she came to

stay with us when I was four. She asked

                                 ....uues and mysteries. Do you
want beans on toast for your tea?'

I thought, 'I'll ask Aunt Primrose when
I see her. I'll ask her what the answer is.'

And, big surprise, I was actually looking
forward to seeing her! I even felt quite
excited about it. There were loads of questions I wanted to ask her. Like: did you
really change colour? Like: what's the
answer to that riddle? Like: why did you
tell Dad that I was special?

Chapter Three

'I'm going to miss my plane,' said Dad through clenched teeth, 'if we don't find her house right NOW.'

'A mile past the fishing village. Then look out for a track to the left and some twisted chimney-pots. That's what she said, isn't it? She says the locals call it Two Sisters Cove but there's no signpost. Typical! I think we're lost!'

But then I saw them over the trees. Four chimney-pots, twisted like candy sticks.

'Just like Aunt Primrose said,' I thought.

'We're not lost, we're there,' I said, from the back seat. 'Turn left, Mum.'

Mum spun the wheel and we went bouncing down a steep, grassy track.

'There's the sea. And look, there's a

There was a padlocked gate across the track. Mum stopped the car. But she kept the engine running.

'Make this quick,' she said to Dad. 'Just hand George over and get away. We'll thank her properly when we get back.'

'We'll bring her a present,' said Dad.

I climbed out of the car and looked at the sparkling waves.

I took a great big lungful of salty sea air.

'I'm going to like it here,' I thought.

Dad strode round, pulled my bag out of the boot and dumped it on the track.

Mum revved the car. 'Hurry up. Look, there she is.'

'Hi!' Dad raised his arm.

There was a person standing in the door of the house. The person waved.

'She looks just the same!' muttered

Mum. 'For heaven's sake, she's even wearing the same tweedy suit. And her hair is still a nightmare!'

Dad clambered over the gate. He had his best suit on. 'Drat!' he said. 'I've got mud on my trousers!' Then he hurried up the track towards Aunt Primrose.

I said, 'Wait for me!' I grabbed my bag and slung it over the gate.

I was just about to climb after it when Mum said: 'Aren't you going to say good-bye to your poor Mumsikins?'

So I went back to the car. ''Bye.'

She leaned out and ruffled my hair. I hate that. And she said, ''Bye, Georgie. Be good. Miss you. Phone you tomorrow.'

Dad was still up at the house, talking to Aunt Primrose.

Mum checked her watch. 'What is he doing?' she fumed. 'He knows we're running late!'

Parp, parp. She gave him two blasts on the car horn. Seagulls flew up from the rocks, squawking like mad.

Dad came walking back down the track and climbed the gate.

He looked really strange, as if he was in

just the same as always.

'She's got pink rubber gloves on,' Dad said.

'Pardon?' said Mum.

'She was wearing big pink rubber gloves, all floppy, like cows' udders. And she said, "Excuse my gloves. I've just been washing my best china, for afternoon tea."'

'Fascinating,' said Mum, revving the car a bit more. 'But you've got a plane to catch.'

Dad still looked dazed. He didn't seem to care any more about catching the plane.

'No, no, but listen,' he said. 'She took off one of her udders. I mean, her rubber gloves. You know, to take the piece of paper with our telephone numbers on it, in case George needs to phone us. She took

15

the glove off and as she was taking the piece of paper her fingertips brushed mine and I felt, I felt –'

Mum began to wind up the window.

'I felt an electric shock,' Dad blurted out. 'A definite electric shock went right up my arm. In fact, it's still tingling!'

Mum didn't say anything for a minute. Then she said, 'I think, after this business trip, that you should take a holiday. I think you've been working too hard.'

Dad climbed into the car.

''Bye, old chap,' he said through the open window. 'Have a whale of a time.'

As the car backed away I could hear them arguing.

'We must remember to phone George tomorrow.'

'Well, I can't phone him. I've got wall-to-wall meetings.'

'Do you think I haven't?'

'Well, someone's got to phone him –'

Then their voices faded away.

I watched the car until I couldn't see it any more. Then I watched the flash of its windows on the main road. Then that disappeared too. They were gone.

Primrose was waiting.

Now I could take a good look at Two Sisters Cove. There were no nice sandy beaches. Just rocks, leading down to the sea. There was a door in the sea-wall, so you could explore the rocks. You could go rock-pooling, if you wanted to. But I thought, '*Hmmm*, think I'll give that a miss.' Those rocks looked dangerous to me – all slippery and black.

There was one pool in the rocks that was bigger than all the rest. It wasn't a nice seaweedy shrimping pool. It was square and black and deep, big enough to swim in. And there were steps, cut from the rock, going down into it.

'What are those hooks for?' I asked myself.

I'd just noticed them. A ring of hooks

like iron claws. They were hammered into a flat bit of rock, next to the pool.

And I was just beginning to think, 'This place is very creepy,' when Aunt Primrose called to me from the house.

'*Cooeee!* George! George dear!'

Her voice was sweet as honey. As soft as doves cooing.

'Coming, Aunt Primrose!' I shouted.

I hurried up the track. My brain was buzzing with all the questions I wanted to ask her. And the most important one of all was: 'What makes me so special?'

'What if Aunt Primrose isn't like I remember?' I began to worry, as I was lugging my bag to the house. 'What if she seems like a stranger?'

But as soon as I saw her up close I thought, 'She's just the same!'

Everything about her checked out. Well, almost everything.

She was quite fat, for a start. Even more like a puffed-up cushion than I remembered. And she had the same frizzy white hair. The make-up was a bit of a shock though – that poppy-red mouth and flour-white face. I thought, 'I don't remember that!' Or the purple Doc Martens boots she had on her feet.

'George, is that really you?' she cried,

rushing up to me. 'My, my, how you've grown! The last time I saw you, you were hardly more than a baby.'

And she squeezed me so hard with her pink rubber gloves that she made me wince.

But it was the best proof. The best proof of all that she was the same Aunt Primrose I remembered. She was making a big fuss of me. Treating me like I was special. Just like she had when I was four years old.

I felt like melted chocolate inside. I couldn't stop grinning a big sloppy grin, even though I was miles too old to be hugged.

'Hello, Aunt Primrose,' I said. 'It's really nice to see you again.'

I'd forgotten what her voice sounded like. It was like a lovely warm bath. So relaxing that all the questions I wanted to ask her drifted right out of my head.

'How about afternoon tea?' said Aunt Primrose. 'Would you like that, George? I know you boys have appetites like gulper fish! It's nothing special, I'm afraid. Just crabsticks and kipper paste sandwiches. Do

crabstick. I've never even *seen* one.

But Aunt Primrose said, 'We shall get on, George. We have lots in common. I might look like an old lady. But I'm not what I seem.'

Her shining eyes looked deep, deep into mine and it was really queer because I felt myself getting woozy. I had to hold on to her so I didn't fall over.

'I've got some urgent things to ask you,' I told her. 'As soon as I remember what they are.'

'Never mind,' she said. 'We've got oceans and oceans of time. Let's snatch a few crabsticks, shall we?'

She patted down her frizzy hair. 'These sea breezes play havoc with your hairstyle,' she said. 'I must look a fright.'

'Oh, no you don't,' I told her. 'You look – beautiful.'

'Do I? Do I, George?' she said. She clasped her pink rubber hands together. She was really delighted.

'You and me, George,' she said, 'are going to be friends. We'll be close as barnacles on a ship's bottom.'

And I could feel myself grinning that big sloppy grin. I just couldn't help it.

As we went inside she let something fly out of her hand. It was a piece of white paper.

'Silly me,' she said.

I jumped up to catch it but it got away. A seagull snatched it, then let it go. It twirled into the sea and was sucked under the waves.

'Never mind,' said Aunt Primrose. 'It was nothing important. Only your parents' telephone numbers. Where you could phone if you needed them. But you won't need them, will you, George?'

She gazed into my eyes for a long, long time.

'No,' I said in a dreamy voice. 'Course

always asking questions. They're like fleas, jumping round in my head. Mrs Perkins says 'How?' and 'Why?' are my favourite words. But I didn't ask any questions just then. I felt weird – sleepy and calm and not curious at all. As if something had shut down my brain.

The kitchen had curtains made out of orange fishing-nets. But that seemed quite normal.

The radio was playing music. As Aunt Primrose clumped past in her purple boots it crackled like mad. She switched it off.

'What rubbish music is nowadays,' she said. 'There's no tune to it. I like a good sea-shanty myself. "Sixteen men on a dead man's chest. Yo-ho-ho and a bottle of rum." Now there's a good tune.

They don't write 'em like that any more.'

And she turned and stared at me with those hypnotizing eyes.

'I like a good sea-shanty myself,' I repeated, dozily. 'They're great. All us kids love them. We play them on our stereos all the time.'

Afternoon tea was normal.

Aunt Primrose took off her rubber gloves. She put on a frilly apron and brought out china cups and silver tea-spoons and napkins and plates.

'I like things to be dainty and ladylike,' she said.

'So do I,' I agreed.

Then, *splat*, she suckered her hand to a plate.

She carried the plate across the room and released it on to the table, with a sound like Velcro ripping. I didn't even blink.

'Thank you, Aunt Primrose,' I said.

She sat down and shook out her napkin and spread it across her knees.

'Do help yourself to a kipper paste sand-

...ich,' she said, 'I'm going to have one.'

I was just going to reach for a sandwich when – *whoosh*, she pounced on them! One arm stretched out and snatched a sandwich and stuffed it into her mouth. *Gulp*, she swallowed it whole.

There was a blur of snatching arms and *gulp, gulp, gulp*, she'd snaffled the entire lot. The plate was empty.

She sat down. She gave a big belch. Then she dabbed at her poppy lips with a napkin, as if nothing had happened.

'Gosh,' I said.

Aunt Primrose swivelled her eyes in my direction.

'Tea?' she said. 'One lump or two? It's just ordinary tea I'm afraid. No Earl Grey or Orange Pekoe. I'm just an ordinary kind of girl.'

'Oh, no you're not,' I blurted out. 'My

mum says you are. But you're not ordinary at all.'

Things happened very quickly. First her voice changed. It wasn't sweet any more. It was deep and booming. It roared like an angry sea.

'Not ordinary?' she boomed. 'Not ordinary? Who DARES say I'm not ordinary?'

She seemed to be swelling. Getting bigger and bigger – I cringed in my seat. *Brring, brring.* Alarm bells were ringing in my sleepy brain. But I couldn't do anything about it. I couldn't move a muscle.

The kitchen was going crazy. The green light on the freezer was flashing on and off. The timer on the microwave went berserk. Aunt Primrose's hair exploded like a giant dandelion clock. Some of it shot clean off her head and floated round the room!

Then very, very slowly, she shrank again. She sat down. She stuck her hair back over the bald bits on her head.

'Silly me,' she said, staring deep into my eyes. 'I almost spoiled our lovely afternoon tea. Just as we were getting on so well. Have a crabstick.'

was hard to see in the dark. When had it got dark?

Aunt Primrose was nibbling a crabstick. She had one suckered to the end of each finger and a teacup suckered to her thumb. I could see her grey wrinkly scalp through her scrappy hair.

But that was absolutely normal.

It seemed the ideal time to ask those questions – the ones that had seemed so important before. I searched around in my brain for them. But there seemed to be nothing in there. Just a lot of clouds. Then I remembered something – something about a riddle. But I couldn't remember what the riddle was.

It didn't seem to matter anyway. I felt so, so sleepy.

'I think,' I told Aunt Primrose, 'I'll have

an early night tonight. Is it night yet?'

'Oh yes,' she said. 'It's been night for a long time now.'

As she showed me up to my bedroom we passed that room again. The door was half-open and I saw steps leading down into the green gloom. What was that noise?

'Is that the sea down there,' I asked Aunt Primrose. 'Can I hear the waves? And what's that funny smell? It smells like the wet fish counter in the supermarket.'

But she turned round and stared into my eyes. And any more questions were sucked right out of my head.

'You can't go in there,' she said, kicking the door shut with her purple boot. 'It's really untidy. I haven't done the dusting.'

So I just stumbled behind her up the stairs.

When she'd gone and I was on my own in my bedroom my brain didn't feel so fuzzy.

I thought, 'This place is weird!' Only I didn't exactly know why and it didn't worry me very much, so I stared out of the window instead.

Primrose. It felt as if I belonged here. It felt as if I'd been here for ever.

I looked out of the other window. It faced inland, over fields of sheep.

Something moved in the moonlit fields.

What was it? I twitched my specs further up my nose and looked a bit closer. What on earth was it?

Something was creeping about among the sheep. A dark, crouching figure. I watched it sliding along by the wire fence. Then lost it in some shadows. Found it again. It was picking something wispy off the wire – it couldn't be Aunt Primrose, could it?

Just as my brain was getting curious there was a terrific rumbling roar.

I dashed back to the other window.

The tide had turned. Two Sisters Cove

wasn't peaceful any more. The sea was like a wild tiger. A massive Hoover seemed to be sucking it up. But it was fighting every inch of the way, clawing at the rocks with foamy fingers, being dragged off, flinging itself back again.

Boom! Boom! Kerrash! The noise was dreadful. Like being inside a giant cement-mixer. I slapped my hands over my ears and wished that it would stop.

N ext morning when I woke up there was sunshine coming through my fishnet curtains.

I jumped out of bed.

I said to myself, 'It's going to be a great day!' But then doubts, like big black crows, started flapping about in my brain.

I thought, uneasily, I ought to be worried about something. I ought to be very, very worried. But that sun looked so bright and cheery . . .

'You probably didn't sleep very well last night,' I told myself. 'Away from home, in a strange bed. You probably had bad dreams or something! But it's daylight now. There's nothing to be scared of in daylight!'

I put my specs on. And the world

stopped being a hazy place. I could see everything clearly.

I thought, 'Bet Mum and Dad will phone today.'

I listened. But the house was very quiet. Maybe Aunt Primrose was still asleep.

I checked my watch. It was blank. The battery seemed to have run out.

I wrapped my orange fishnet duvet around me and shuffled over to the window. Every time I moved, fish scales fell out of my duvet on to the floor like silver confetti.

I peeped out of the window at Two Sisters Cove. The sky was striped pale pink and grey. It must be very early. No wonder Aunt Primrose wasn't up yet.

The tide was out and the rocks were dry.

'I'm going to go fishing in that big square pool,' I decided. 'Right after breakfast.'

But someone else had got there before me.

It was Aunt Primrose in her tweedy suit and purple Doc Martens. She was just standing there, by the side of the pool. What had she seen? She was staring at one spot. Her eyes were gleaming. Then,

head had disappeared up to her neck. Like an ostrich with its head in the sand. Only her head was under the water.

'No one can do that,' I thought. 'I couldn't do that. She must be made of elastic!'

She seemed to have stretched herself like a periscope. Now her head was swivelling round underwater. What was she looking for?

Seconds went by. One, two, three, four, five, six.

I started getting worried.

'Aunt Primrose!' I yelled out of the window, even though she couldn't hear me.

Minutes went by. She still hadn't come up for air. I couldn't even see any bubbles.

Ages went by. I started chewing at

my duvet. But I just got a mouthful of fishbones.

'You'll drown!' I shouted through the window. 'Come up! Come up!'

I felt awful. Like I used to feel when I had asthma attacks, when I was little. I wished I had an inhaler with me. *Gasp, gasp* . . . I couldn't breathe. I felt as if I was drowning too.

'Do something,' my brain shrieked at me. 'She's got her head trapped in the seaweed!'

I flung my fishing-net off my shoulders and went racing downstairs in my boxer shorts. I didn't even stop to put on my shoes.

I rushed to the kitchen and out of the back door. The sea-wall stopped me. There was a door in it somewhere. But where?

Frantically I rushed along the wall.

'There! There it is!'

The door had a big iron ring for a handle. I turned it and ran out on to the rocks.

I was skidding on seaweed, slicing my feet on barnacles, but I didn't care.

pool. It was clear as glass. But floating up towards me were some white wispy strands . . .

'Oh no,' I thought. 'It's her hair. She's drowned. She's drowned!'

I just couldn't bear it. She'd said I was special. She'd made a fuss of me. And now she'd drowned.

I plunged my arm into the water and grabbed hold of the hair. But there was no body on the end of it. I put my face close to the water and peered through it. It was trembling down there, with light and shadows.

My breath whooshed out of my body in a great big *phew!* of relief. She wasn't in the pool. There were some fish flickering down there. But no one in a tweedy suit or purple boots.

35

'Wonder where she is?'

But she hadn't drowned. That was all that mattered.

I just sat for a bit, huddled up on the rocks. Now the panic was over I felt really cold and shaky.

Maybe I'd made a mistake. Maybe she hadn't been under the water as long as I thought. Time didn't seem to have any meaning in Two Sisters Cove.

The sun came creeping over the rocks and warmed me up. My brain seemed to be warming up too. I felt better. And I started remembering things. I remembered the riddle, for a start: *The more you take, the more you leave behind.*

'I must ask Aunt Primrose the answer to that,' I thought.

But I was remembering other things as well. They made me shiver, even in the warm sun. They were scary, sinister things.

Velcro hands? Who had Velcro hands that stuck to plates? Whose hair exploded if you called them not ordinary?

I was just starting to get really worried.

Then something, I don't know what, made

masses of woolly hair. Even more of it than usual.

'Wait a minute!' I thought. 'Aunt Primrose looks like a freak! She looks like something out of a horror film!'

My heart started to pound: *boom, boom, boom, boom, boom.*

But then she opened the window and leaned out.

'Cooee, George!' she called in that syrupy voice which seemed to suck all my willpower away. 'Breakfast is ready. What would you like? Kippers? Kedgeree? Or there's always crabsticks.'

Her big eyes glowed like traffic-lights. They looked deep into mine. I couldn't take my eyes away. She didn't blink once. She couldn't. She hadn't got any eyelids.

I'd only just noticed that. But I wasn't a bit surprised. Or worried.

I waved back. 'I'm coming, Aunt Primrose.'

I got up from the rocks and started stumbling towards the house.

I didn't think she was a freak any more. 'She's an ordinary person,' I kept telling myself in a robot voice. 'Just a perfectly ordinary person.'

I stumbled back through the door in the sea-wall. Aunt Primrose was washing up at the kitchen sink.

'Have a crabstick,' she said, handing one to me with her pink rubber gloves. 'I've already had my breakfast.'

Then she turned her back to me and plunged her gloves into the soapy bubbles.

Clack, clack, clack. I could hear my teeth chattering.

'Why am I standing here?' I thought. 'On these cold stone tiles, in my boxer shorts?'

Then suddenly I remembered. I remembered the shock of that wispy hair floating up through the water.

'I was scared you'd drowned,' I told her.

'I ran out to the pool to rescue you. I didn't even stop to put any clothes on.'

Aunt Primrose turned round. Even though I was half in a trance, I could see a strange change in her. Her eyes, chilly and black as the deepest oceans, seemed to melt to a warmer blue. She looked at me, just for a second, as if she was really moved.

When she spoke, her voice sounded kind. 'Don't worry,' she said. 'I won't drown. Though it was a near thing in the Arctic once, when I got scooped off the bottom by a Russian trawler. But I won't drown in the bathing pool.'

'The bathing pool,' I repeated, dreamily.

'That's right, George. It was cut out of the rock a hundred years ago. To make a safe place for ladies to bathe. Didn't you see the steps and the hooks?'

'Hooks?' I couldn't seem to do anything but repeat what she said. My head seemed to be full of cotton wool.

Aunt Primrose sighed. She said, still kindly, 'A bit slow today, aren't we, my little sea-slug? Never mind, can't be helped.

I followed her through the kitchen, to that mysterious door with the green glow behind it. She pushed the door wide open. 'Careful,' she warned me. 'The steps are slippery.' Then she disappeared.

I didn't want to go down into that green glow.

'Come inside, George,' said a voice, soft as a feather bed. 'There's nothing to be afraid of. Come and meet my precious.'

I didn't seem to have any choice. My feet had a mind of their own. They went down the steps. And I had to go with them.

'Yuk!'

My hand touched something squidgy on the walls. It was a blob of jelly – a closed-up sea anemone.

Green light rippled around me. *Drip, drip, drip*. Water was trickling down the walls. All I could do was stare and stare, with my mouth hanging open. We were in a kind of cellar. But it wasn't a cellar really. It was like being at the bottom of a giant rock pool. The rocky walls were covered with seaweed and blue mussel shells and barnacles.

The light came in through slits, high up in the wall, filled with thick green glass.

Pop! I jumped a mile. But it was only a fat seaweed pod, squishing into slime under my feet.

I twitched my specs further up my nose. I peered into the green gloom.

'Where are you, Aunt Primrose?'

'Here I am.'

She was standing by a large glass fish-tank. There were fish-tanks on stands everywhere. And they all had wire mesh on top. So what was inside them couldn't get out.

'That's a puffer fish,' said Aunt Primrose, pointing through the glass.

A little fish with a mouth like a kiss blew himself up into a big football.

'And here's my jellyfish collection.'

Some jellyfish drifted by like ghosts.

you like to see them, George? Flying fish, lantern fish, deep-sea jellyfish, pink and green and gold like lovely water lilies . . .'

'Oh yes,' I said dreamily. 'I'd love to see all those.'

'Would you, George? Would you? Then you shall see something now. You shall see one of the great wonders of the ocean.'

She tapped on the glass of the next tank.

'And here,' she whispered, 'is my precious.'

Behind the glass I saw arms, writhing about. I could see a bulging bald head. And two eyes that looked horribly human.

'Isn't he beautiful?' breathed Aunt Primrose.

'Oh, yes,' I said, in my dozy voice. 'He's lovely.'

The octopus blushed a crimson colour.

Wavy lines appeared on Aunt Primrose's neck. They were pink and purple. Then the octopus replied with jumping blue polka-dots. They were talking to each other in octopus language. Having a conversation.

I knew what they were doing. And I wasn't a bit surprised. It all seemed – perfectly normal. Like chatting to your mates in the school playground.

'He's a deadly predator,' said Aunt Primrose proudly. 'See his beak? That can bite through steel cables. See those suckers? They can stamp circles out of a killer whale. Like a biscuit cutter through pastry! And he's cunning, my precious. He can fall on his prey like a parachute. Or shoot out ink that makes an octopus shape – so they think he's where he's not. Or hide under sand with just his eyes showing and grab 'em when they swim by. Wonderful!'

'Wonderful,' I agreed in my robot voice.

'I'll give you a tour,' said Aunt Primrose, 'of my little collection. But we haven't much time. This cellar floods with water

ing through the underground tunnels. See the water already coming up through cracks and holes in the floor.

Aunt Primrose moved on to another tank.

'Meet George,' she said to whatever was in there.

A massive eel-shape squirmed in the ooze. Aunt Primrose lifted the mesh and scratched its back.

'He's sulking,' she said.

Suddenly she dashed back, lifted the mesh and pulled the puffer fish out of its tank. She threw it in with the eel.

'Dinner-time,' she said softly.

The puffer fish blew itself up in a panic. It looked like a stripy black and yellow beachball.

But the eel didn't move.

Aunt Primrose shrugged. 'Oh well, please yourself,' she said. And she lobbed the puffer fish back into its own tank. It shrivelled like a popped balloon, until it was normal size.

I saw all this. My eyes took in every detail. But I saw it all through a groggy haze. Like when you're very, very tired. Or you've just woken up from having gas at the dentist's.

'Such a pity you can't see my eel in action,' Aunt Primrose was saying. 'He can shock you with 300 volts. Magnificent! The Romans kept them in ponds and fed their runaway slaves to them. Excellent after-dinner entertainment!'

I could feel something sloshing around my feet. I looked down. The cellar floor was flooding with water. Sea anemones were springing open, like a field of orange daisies.

Aunt Primrose was annoyed. 'Tut, tut. We'll have to go and my tour has only just started. There's a cobra shark over there. Very rare. Almost extinct. From the deepest of deep abysses. Don't look at him,

46

'Then,' she said, 'when you're completely at their mercy, they POUNCE!'

'*Aargh!*' I leapt backwards and crashed
into a tank. 'Ow! I've cut my hand on the
wire.'

'Sorry,' said Aunt Primrose, sweetly.
'Didn't mean to scare you.'

I sucked the blood off my cut hand.
'Ouch, that stings.'

But the pain had woken something
inside my brain. Those bells were going
berserk! Ringing inside my head like a
fire-engine.

I looked around as if I was seeing everything for the first time. What was I doing
down here? In this spooky, seaweedy
cellar?

From a tank in the corner came a
scratching sound.

'What's in there?' I pointed at the tank. 'Why is it covered up?'

Questions were beginning to buzz round in my brain.

Aunt Primrose glanced towards the tank. It had a blue plastic sheet over it so you couldn't see inside. 'Oh, that,' she said, in a casual voice. 'That's empty. There's no water in it.'

'But I heard –' I started to say.

'You heard nothing!' said Aunt Primrose as we splashed towards the stairs.

But I was busy thinking my own private thoughts. 'I did,' I decided. 'I'm sure I did.'

At the top of the steps I turned round to wait for her.

What on earth was she doing? Horrified, I saw sea water gushing in. With it came glittery fish. I saw Aunt Primrose snatch one out of the water. She let it flap for a minute, stuck fast to her hand.

She wasn't going to –? Oh yes, she was. My eyes opened wide in shock as she flipped the fish into her mouth. And crunched it up alive, even the bones.

Then she looked up at me with her

traffic-light eyes. She stared and stared.

from the big covered tank went on and on and on. Then she shut the cellar door behind us and I couldn't hear it any more.

Chapter Seven

'What happy times,' said Aunt Primrose, as she turned a page in the old photograph album. 'Carefree times when I was just an ordinary little girl.'

This time I didn't contradict her. Deep in my jelly brain, I remembered that it wasn't a good idea to contradict Aunt Primrose when she said she was ordinary.

So I said, 'You were ever so pretty.'

'Ahhhh!' She gave a hiss of pleasure. 'I was, wasn't I?'

We were sitting at the kitchen table. It was already afternoon but I couldn't remember where the hours had flown. I thought it was still Monday. But I wasn't even sure about that. Since I'd come to

we used

tumes. Look!' she said in a sharp voice. 'You aren't looking!'

I tried to make myself concentrate on the picture. It was an old black and white photo. And there was a family in it, sitting on the rocks by the bathing pool. Pa in a straw hat, Ma in a big floppy sunhat. And little Aunt Primrose with her hair like Alice in Wonderland, in a frilly frock and white button-up shoes. And behind them a jolly striped tent like a teepee, tied down to the iron hooks.

'It always seemed to be summer then,' Aunt Primrose was saying. 'And I was everyone's favourite. Pa called me his little princess. Look at my golden hair. Everyone loved me. Ahhh! Long-lost happy days!'

She gave a long, sad sigh. She took off her rubber gloves and stroked the photo.

51

She seemed to have forgotten all about me. She hadn't stared into my eyes for a long, long time . . .

My brain started to wake up.

'So that's what the iron hooks are for,' I told myself. 'For putting a tent up.' Somehow I'd thought they had a much more sinister purpose.

The photo wasn't sinister either. It was – just ordinary. It was a sunny day. Everyone was smiling. The bathing pool looked liked a shiny mirror.

Except – except there was *something* odd about the photo. I tried to study it but my mind was still foggy.

Got it! Someone had been snipped out. There was a neat, person-shaped hole right in the middle of the photo. That wasn't ordinary. I frowned and turned the page. The next one had a piece cut out of it too.

I opened my mouth to ask Aunt Primrose a question. 'Why –?'

Burrp, burrp!

'Telephone!' yelled Aunt Primrose as she leapt up, knocking the album on to the floor.

'...my mum!' I cried, and I

...gone.

A pain, like electricity, shot through my body when she pushed me. The pain fizzled out and left just a tingling feeling. But something had happened to my brain. The shock had jump-started it. Thoughts were fizzing around in there. Just like they used to do.

I picked up the album. And when I did, a shower of little girls fell out of the back of it. I scooped them up and spread them out on the table. They'd all been cut out of photographs. And they were all the same little girl. They were all Aunt Primrose.

'Two Aunt Primroses?' I thought. It didn't make sense.

I turned the pages of the album and, like doing jigsaws, I fitted the little girls into the holes in the photographs. So now each one had two Aunt Primroses in it. Like seeing double.

'Is it trick photography or what?' I thought.

I twitched my specs up my nose and looked closer. 'A-ha!'

I'd found the answer. I could see that the little girl snipped from the photos wasn't Aunt Primrose at all. At first she looked the same. But now I could see some differences. In this photo the second little girl had different shoes.

I turned the page. In this one her socks were falling down. And in all the photos she wasn't as pretty as Aunt Primrose. She had golden hair. She had a friendly, smiley face. But she didn't look like a fairytale princess in the way Aunt Primrose did.

Those warning bells in my head were as loud as cathedral bells!

I flipped through the album again and took the mystery girl out of the photographs. Something told me that Aunt Primrose wouldn't like to see her there when she got back.

... the cut-out pieces into the

telephone.

'Was it my mum?'

'No,' said Aunt Primrose. 'It was a wrong number.'

'But –'

She stared into my eyes like a cobra shark.

'Isn't she weird-looking?' I thought.

For the second time, it hit me how gruesome her white make-up was. It was plastered on, thick as Christmas cake icing. And her hair! It was scraggy and tatty. It exploded like dandelion clocks! It floated in pools!

I thought, 'That's not her own hair. That's fake hair!'

Her eyes glowed white hot. She gave me a triple blast of her cobra-shark stare.

Instantly my head went all woozy. 'Oh no,' I thought. 'Not again.'

So I took my glasses off.

I've got bad eyesight. It's really bad in my left eye. When I take off my specs everything goes fuzzy on that side. So I turned my face to the right. Straight away Aunt Primrose became a white blur. I could see her red mouth moving. But I couldn't see her stare.

And guess what happened? I didn't have a cotton-wool brain any more. It stayed sharp. It stayed on full alert!

'Aunt Primrose,' I said. 'You remember that riddle you told me once – *the more you take, the more you leave behind*? What's the answer to that riddle? I've been meaning to ask you ever since I got here. I mean, you did ask me that riddle, didn't you?'

Aunt Primrose looked blank. Just for a second. Then she lisped in a voice all soft and buttery: 'Oh yes, I did ask you that widdle. I wemember it now. But would you believe it, I can't wemember the answer. The answer to that widdle has gone wight out of my head. It's not important, is it?'

I turned my face sideways. When I
wouldn't have forgotten the answer. She
wouldn't have said it wasn't important. I
felt quite sure about that.

'What's going on?' I thought, squinting
out of my left eye at the red and white
smudge across the table.

And suddenly I felt very, very unsafe
indeed.

Chapter Eight

I was on my own in my bedroom. At last I could put my specs back on. All day everything around me had been fuzzy. But it wasn't fuzzy inside my head any more.

I looked out of the window at Two Sisters Cove. The tide was out. The bathing pool glittered in the moonlight. There were crowds of stars in the sky. It was nearly as bright as day.

I listened. The house was very, very still. Aunt Primrose must have gone to bed.

I was really worried about her. I'd decided she was very weird indeed. I'd decided I was scared of her. And why hadn't Mum and Dad phoned? And what day was it? My mind was like a washing-machine with questions tumbling round and round.

Or was I just going crazy?

But there was a problem even more urgent than all of these. I was starving. My stomach was going, 'Feed me!' It needed something besides crabsticks. I'd had crabsticks every day for breakfast, lunch and tea. There must be something else in those kitchen cupboards. Some biscuits. Or even some crisps.

'They're probably prawn cocktail flavour,' I muttered to myself.

But it didn't matter. I had to have FOOD!

So I made a plan. I was going to:

1. Creep down to the kitchen and search for FOOD.
2. Creep back to the bedroom and scoff FOOD.

3. Worry about whether or not I was going
   crazy.

I opened my bedroom door a crack. It
went *squeak*!

Oh no, I thought. 'She'll hear it.'

I held my breath. But nothing stirred in
the house.

So I tiptoed along the upstairs landing.

Then I heard it – a strange, shushing
sound. Like the surf on a distant shore.
Like listening to a sea-shell.

It was Aunt Primrose, singing to herself.

I should have crept straight past her
open bedroom door. But I couldn't. I had
to stop and look inside.

She was sitting in front of a mirror,
combing her wispy hair. She had her back
to me. She seemed really happy and peaceful, singing a weird little song.

'*Under the sea*,' she was crooning,
'*Georgie and me.*
Oh, how happy we shall be,
Under the sea.'

And I nearly stepped inside the door.

Then something terrible happened.

Aunt Primrose's comb got stuck in her hair.

'Bother,' she said.

She gave it a tug. Then another.

And a big tuft of hair came right out of her head.

She went bananas!

'*Aaaaaargh!*' she cried, in a shriek that rattled the windows.

I cringed back into the shadows.

'This sheep's wool is useless!' she screamed into the mirror. 'It won't stay glued on. It's a total waste of time collecting it!'

And suddenly, she was yanking it all off her head in great big handfuls. Her scalp was grey and baggy like elephant skin.

'I'm sick!' she shrieked. 'Sick and tired of pretending! Sick of being ordinary! Sick of afternoon tea!'

She got up out of her chair.

'I've changed my plans!' she cried. 'I can't stay here a minute longer! I'm going back right now!'

And in one horrific moment, with a noise like a whoopee cushion, she started to collapse.

Like a puffer fish blowing out air, her plump body shrivelled. Her tweedy suit fell to the floor. Her white make-up cracked like the ice on a pond and fell off.

And, after the shrinking, all that was left on the carpet was a horrid, grey wrinkly thing squirming around. It had a massive bulgy head and body and skinny, writhing arms and legs.

But it still had Aunt Primrose's big red lips. It had her mega-intelligent eyes. And two of the tentacles still had her purple boots on the end.

'Ahhhhhh!' The Thing on the carpet gave a great sigh of relief. 'That's better,' it said to itself. 'Like taking a corset off.

The Thing sniffed the air. It waved two tentacles, with suckers on the end.

'What can I smell?' it hissed. 'Is that you, George? Come closer, George.'

Then it started to croon its terrible song.

'Under the sea,
Georgie and me.
Oh, how happy we shall be,
Under the sea.'

My brain was screaming at me: 'Run, George! Run!'

With a superhuman effort, I made my legs walk. I took one tottering step. Then a slithery tentacle shot out and curled round my ankle.

'Come closer, George,' said the Thing on the carpet. 'I've got something to tell you. I'm going back to the sea. But I've grown fond of you, George, while I've been here. So, guess what? I'm taking you with me!'

The Thing was reeling me in like a fish on a line. I stumbled towards it.

'Don't look in its eyes!' my brain was babbling. 'Don't look in its eyes!'

'Just think, George,' hissed the Thing. 'When you grow up, you will be Lord of the Oceans. Dolphins will be your servants. You can hitch a ride on a humpback whale!'

With another superhuman effort, I managed to twitch off my specs.

'No!' I screamed, in a panic. 'No! I'm not coming with you!'

The tentacle tightened round my ankle. But I wrenched myself free. I staggered down the stairs.

'Hide!' my brain told me. 'Hide! Hide!'

I took a quick look behind me. The Thing wasn't following. I hardly knew where I was going, what I was doing. I half-ran, half-fell down the cellar steps, and crouched in that spooky green glow under

...ng out tank, gasping for breath and

Chapter Nine

I looked up at the tank. I put my specs back on. I still couldn't see inside it – it was covered with a blue plastic sheet. But the scratching noise had stopped.

I peered round the cellar. It was like being at the bottom of the ocean. Soupy green moonlight was coming through the windows. There were fishy eyes and gleaming fangs everywhere.

But the Thing wasn't coming down the steps. The door at the top stayed closed where I'd slammed it shut behind me. Maybe I was safe here for a bit. Maybe the Thing didn't know where I was hiding.

Suddenly, the legs of the tank started to tremble.

'What's going on?' I thought in a panic.

And I scuttled like a crab from underneath, just as the blue plastic sheet slid off, *flop*, in a big heap on the floor.

I had to look into the tank. I just had to.

My hand went flying up to my mouth. 'Oh no!'

The tank was full of water. It had wire mesh on top of it, weighted down with rocks.

And inside the tank, curled up like a giant pink water-baby, was another Aunt Primrose!

For a few seconds, my brain went blank with shock. I just stared and stared, my mouth hanging open.

She had that green and golden bathing suit on – the one she'd bought in London. Her white hair floated like seaweed round her head. Her eyes were wide open. They were looking straight at me.

'Its *my* Aunt Primrose – it's the *real* Aunt Primrose,' I whispered to myself.

And she was dead. Drowned in a tank of water.

My knees started to crumple. Then something astonishing happened. Bubbles came out of her mouth! They fizzed up and burst on the surface of the tank.

I couldn't believe it. I had to hang on to the tank to stop myself falling. She's alive, I thought.

Her lips started to move. More bubbles came out, a whole crowd of them. She was trying to tell me something. But I couldn't make out the words.

'What?' I pleaded. 'What?'

'Get – me – out,' said the mouth. And Aunt Primrose's pink hand waved upwards, towards the mesh.

I stretched up and pushed off some rocks. They went crashing to the floor.

'*Shhhhh! Shhhh!*' I warned myself, with a scared look at the cellar door. But nothing came slithering down the steps.

I heaved off the last few rocks and
[illegible]

bubbles.

I pulled back the wire mesh and Aunt
Primrose uncurled from the tank. She
stood up, streaming with water.

Then she climbed over the edge. 'Thank
goodness you found me, George,' she
said. 'It was getting awfully cramped in
there.'

She gave me a hug. It was a damp, seaweedy, salty sort of hug. But I felt safe
straight away. Really, truly safe this time.

I checked her eyes. They weren't cobra-
shark eyes. They were wise and kind. I
knew for certain that I'd found the real
Aunt Primrose. And that the Thing
upstairs was an imposter.

Questions were fighting to get out of my
mouth.

'Who's that upstairs pretending to be you?'

'That's my twin sister, Violet,' said Aunt Primrose. 'She disguised herself as me. But she's a Sea Hag, really.'

'Why didn't you drown? How could you breathe in that water?'

'I've got gills, of course,' said Aunt Primrose, in the same matter-of-fact voice. She pushed aside her draggly hair. Behind her ear there were four slits in her neck.

I felt dizzy. My brain just wouldn't take it in. My knees started to crumple all over again. Aunt Primrose caught me. 'Sit down,' she said. 'You've had lots of awful shocks. You've had a dreadful time! Sit down and I'll explain everything.'

I smiled gratefully at her. I let myself sink down to the cellar floor among the blobby sea anemones.

Aunt Primrose sat down beside me.

'She wants to take me away,' I told her. 'She said she likes me and . . .'

'Oh dear,' interrupted Aunt Primrose. 'She didn't say she *likes* you, did she?'

I nodded miserably.

'Don't worry,' said Aunt Primrose. 'I'll

Primrose.'

'I know,' I told her with a deep, deep sigh of relief.

I felt safe with her. Safe from the Sea Hag.

But I still felt bewildered. I still didn't know what was going on. There were so many weird things, so many extraordinary things happening all around me, that it seemed like the most important question in the world.

'Why am I so special?' I asked the real Aunt Primrose.

Chapter Ten

'I'll tell you why you're special,' said the real Aunt Primrose, as we sat huddled up on the slimy cellar floor. 'But before I do, there are other things that you must understand. Things about your family. About my twin sister, Violet, the Sea Hag.'

I was going to interrupt to ask about the riddle. 'Tell me the answer, please!' I was going to beg her. But her voice sounded so solemn that it drove the riddle clean out of my head.

'Does my sister know you're down here?' asked Aunt Primrose. 'If she doesn't, we're safe here until the next high tide.'

'I don't know. I ran away! I don't *think* she knows where I am.' I gripped Aunt

Primrose's arm. 'But I saw her, Aunt Prim-

proudly, as if there was a world of difference. 'There hasn't been a Sea Hag in our
family since sixteen forty-two. We thought
they'd died out.'

'But she's got tentacles,' I said, shivering
just thinking about it. 'She's got tentacles
with suckers on them.'

'Yes, she has. But she can also stun you
like an electric eel. Hypnotize you like a
cobra shark. Blow herself up into a puffer
fish, change colour like an octopus –'

'You can change colour,' I interrupted
her. 'I saw you once – that time you came
to stay.'

'Did you?' said Aunt Primrose, smiling.
'I thought there was someone watching.
Yes, I can do that. But that's nothing – it
runs in the family. I've got gills too. Only

73

a few of us have those. But I'm not a Sea Hag. A Sea Hag is a magnificent creature! More powerful than any octopus or shark. She can do things that all of them can do – and more. She can grow new sets of teeth like a shark. She can grow new arms and legs like a starfish. I'm her sister – and even I don't know the true extent of her powers. She *may* even be immortal.'

'But how did she get like that? Was she born a freak?'

'A freak?' Aunt Primrose sounded really shocked. 'Where did you get that idea? She's a Sea Hag. She's the Eighth Wonder of the World. She certainly is not a freak.'

'Sorry,' I apologized. 'I didn't mean to be rude – but was she born a Sea Hag, then?'

'Oh, no,' said Aunt Primrose. 'When we were born, she was quite ordinary. An ordinary beautiful little girl. Violet was the beautiful twin. And I was, well, the plain one.'

'I saw photographs,' I told her excitedly. 'She cut you out of them.'

74

And I dug in my pocket for the snipped-

'Yes,' said Aunt Primrose. 'I'm afraid it
is. But look, I'll start at the beginning. I'll
explain about our family. And then you'll
understand.'

In the tunnels under the cellar there was
the sound of sea water. But it was only a
gentle shushing.

'The tide's coming in,' said Aunt Primrose. 'But we're safe here for a little while
yet.'

As I had when I was four years old, I
curled up in the crook of her arm and
waited for the story to begin.

'Our family,' said Aunt Primrose, 'has
never been ordinary. In the old days they
said it was a curse. But now I think they'd
call it genetic. Anyway, you know that
things run in families – special things, like
being able to waggle your ears or lick your

nose with your tongue or crack your knuckles?'

I nodded. 'My friend can waggle his ears. And his dad can do it. And his grandad.'

'Well, special things run in our family too. But they're all sort of *fishy* things. What I mean,' said Aunt Primrose tactfully, 'is that some of us, from time to time, turn out to be a little bit like sea creatures. I mean, only a little bit – just webbed toes like my father had, or changing colour, or having slime glands or a fin or two. Nothing much. But then my twin sister changed into a Sea Hag. And that was a different thing altogether.'

'But why?' I asked her. 'How did it all start?'

'What, you mean our family being like sea creatures? Well,' Aunt Primrose shrugged, 'who knows? Why can some people waggle their ears? It's a mystery really. All I know is, it's been going on for generations. We were always a seafaring family, the sea in our blood and all that. And there was some talk, hundreds of years ago, about one of us taking a seal-woman

thought the fishy genes were getting
weaker. I mean, it's been ages since anyone
had slime glands. So my sister Violet
changing into a Sea Hag was quite a
surprise.'

At last, I found some words. 'So when
did she start to change?'

'When she was eleven. That's when it
always happens. I didn't get gills till then.
Violet got gills like me, and a few fins. But
she didn't stop. She just went on changing.
Poor Violet.'

'Poor Violet?' I repeated. I didn't feel at
all sorry for the Sea Hag.

'Yes, it was very sad. You see, she wasn't
a bit pleased. When we were little she was
the pretty one. She was a bit vain I suppose, and spoiled. But you couldn't help
loving her. Everybody did. Everyone

invited her to parties. She had lots of admirers –'

'Do you mean boyfriends?' I asked, amazed. 'Didn't they mind about her being a Sea Hag?'

'They didn't know. Not at first. She disguised it very well. She combed her golden hair over her gills. She wore white gloves all the time.'

'To hide her suckers.'

'That's right. But the older she got, the more she changed. Her golden hair started falling out. Her white skin grew grey and tough, like a whale. It got harder and harder to hide what was happening. And one dreadful day when she was seventeen –' Here Aunt Primrose stopped and shook her head, sorrowfully.

'What happened? Tell me what happened!'

'It was a beautiful summer's day – fifty years ago. And Violet was in the tent by the bathing pool. She was getting changed. And her young fiancé, the boy she was going to marry, went creeping over the rocks to surprise her. He called out,

"Cooeee, Violet, my darling!" He peeped

went into a monastery the very next day.
And Violet was broken-hearted.'

'Gosh!' I said.

'And after that, Violet became very bitter and vengeful. She blamed me. She said I was jealous because I wasn't pretty and had no admirers. She said I'd told her fiancé her terrible secret. But I hadn't,' said Aunt Primrose. 'I loved Violet more than anything. I wanted her to be happy.'

A tear sparkled on Aunt Primrose's cheek.

'But she was never happy again,' she said. 'She just wanted to be ordinary. She didn't want any special powers. She stayed in her bedroom and wouldn't see anyone. She stayed there for days and days. Then, one night, at high tide, something came slithering down the stairs. It was Violet.

She'd become a full-blown Sea Hag. We watched from the window. She slithered across the rocks, waved a tentacle at us and disappeared into the waves.'

Aunt Primrose sniffed bravely and wiped her tears away.

'And I never saw her again until the day your father phoned me. When she turned up for afternoon tea. I thought she'd changed. I thought she'd accepted being a Sea Hag. I even thought she wanted us to be friends. But she didn't. She stunned me with an electric shock. Put me in that tank. She said, 'I'm going to be ordinary. I'm going to be like everyone else!' But she can never be ordinary,' said Aunt Primrose. 'No matter how hard she tries. She's a Sea Hag. She's different.'

'She's got fishing-nets all over the place,' I told Aunt Primrose. 'On the windows, on the beds. It looks really weird.'

Aunt Primrose tut-tutted sadly. 'She steals them from trawlers,' she explained. 'She's got a grudge against deep-sea trawlers. I don't know why.'

Under the cellar floor the shushing noise

had turned to sloshing. In the tanks things

the oceans of the world — the Arctic, the
Atlantic, the Pacific. Under the polar ice-
cap. Down in the deepest abysses. Time
means nothing to a Sea Hag. But wherever
she's been, she must have been very lonely.
As far as I know, she's the only Sea Hag
in existence.'

For a minute I felt really sorry for
the Sea Hag, under the oceans of the
world, all alone. I sighed and shook my
head.

Then I remembered she wanted to take
me with her.

'How can she take me with her?' I cried
to Aunt Primrose. 'I'd drown, wouldn't I?'

'Not necessarily,' said Aunt Primrose,
mysteriously.

And she was going to tell me more, when
we both heard the noise.

It came from the top of the cellar steps – a sort of shuffling, slithery kind of noise.

It made the hairs tingle on the back of my neck.

'It's her!' I whispered to Aunt Primrose. 'She knows where I am!'

'I thought she might,' said Aunt Primrose. 'She doesn't miss a thing. She's got built-in radar.'

I thought I heard a tiny tremble in her voice.

'Could she beat you in a fight? Is she more powerful than you?' I asked Aunt Primrose, although I'd already guessed the answer.

'She much more powerful,' said Aunt Primrose. 'She's got the powers of a giant squid, a Portuguese man o' war, a cobra shark. And heaven knows what else. But I've only got the powers of a cuttlefish.'

'Oh dear,' I said. 'And she's in a very bad mood as well.'

It made me shiver just *thinking* about her in her bedroom. Wild with rage, ripping her sheep's wool hair out in handfuls.

I twitched my specs up my nose and

gazed into the blackness at the top of the

remembering the cobra shark. We might as well give up now. We haven't got a chance. She's going to beat you. And take me away with her to the bottom of the deepest, darkest ocean!'

'Don't talk like that, George,' said Aunt Primrose with a sudden fierce look in her eyes. 'You're special. Always remember that. And we special people are used to rough seas. People think we're drowning. Then we pop up, waving! We're full of surprises!'

I tried to be brave. I gave a weedy little cheer. 'Yay!'

I felt a bit better after that. But I still didn't have enough faith. How can a little old lady with the powers of a cuttlefish defeat a mighty Sea Hag?

But Aunt Primrose was already fighting

back. Puffing with the effort, she was lifting up a stone slab in the cellar floor.

'Help me, George. There's a tunnel under here. I didn't want to risk it. But there's no choice now.'

I helped her heave the slab to one side. Underneath was a deep well.

'*Gulp!*' I said when I peered into it. At the bottom you could hear the sea gurgling, like water in a plughole.

'I can't get down there. The tide's coming in. I don't have gills like you.'

'It's our only way out,' said Aunt Primrose. 'Unless you want to go up those steps and face the Sea Hag.'

'Come on, George,' called Aunt Primrose from somewhere under the cellar floor. 'We haven't much time!'

I peered again into the dark well. I'd taken my specs off and put them in my pocket, for safety. Aunt Primrose's face was just a white moon shape.

'Lower yourself down,' she said. 'And before you go underwater take a big breath and I'll do the rest.'

I groaned out loud. 'I don't want to do this,' I thought. 'I really do NOT want to do this!'

But I was alone now in the cellar. And at the top of the steps the Sea Hag was waiting, with her cobra-shark eyes and horrible snaky arms.

I could hear it! Hear her soft, siren song. It was calling to me.

'Under the sea,
Georgie and me.
Oh, how happy we shall be . . .'

'Don't listen!' Aunt Primrose shouted from the dark hole.

I slapped my hands over my ears, so I couldn't hear the song any more. I leaned forward to look into the hole. It made me feel sick and dizzy.

'Don't be afraid,' came Aunt Primrose's voice. 'Trust me.'

So I lowered myself into the tunnel.

'Ow!' Sharp barnacles scraped my hands. Seaweed stroked my face.

My feet kicked out. There was no bottom. My hands were slipping on the slimy walls . . .

Then, *splosh*, I was up to my neck in the cold sea. It was sucking me down!

But even through my panic I remembered what Aunt Primrose had told me. 'Take a big breath.' So I did.

And the water closed over my head.

Dumped on the rocks outside in a soggy heap, gasping for breath, coughing up loads of salty water.

'Are you all right, George?'

I shook the water out of my hair and forced my stinging eyes to open. Then I felt in my shirt pocket. Good, my specs were safe. With trembling fingers, I put them back on.

And there was Aunt Primrose in the water. Curving through the waves as graceful as a seal. Behind her the sky was in layers like a liquorice allsort – pink, grey, white. Dawn was breaking.

'I'm, I'm all right – I think,' I spluttered.

I felt a bit dizzy though. And the roaring in my ears was taking ages to go away. But I stumbled to my feet. The sea foamed round my shoes. I backed away, up the rocks, and almost fell over an iron hook. I was right beside the bathing pool.

Aunt Primrose came rolling up the rocks on the next wave. She flopped about for a bit, then heaved herself to her feet.

'What happened just now?' I asked her in a dazed voice. 'I went through that tunnel like a rocket. How did I do that?'

Aunt Primrose smiled, modestly. 'That was me,' she said. 'I pulled you along. I wasn't sure I could still do that.'

'Do what?'

'Jet propulsion. It's a cuttlefish talent. You suck water in, then shoot it out at the other end of your body. And, *whoosh*, you're jet-propelled. You can whizz through the sea at amazing speeds. Most exhilarating.'

'Gosh!' I said, my mind boggling. 'You mean, you suck water through your mouth?'

'Yes.'

'And then you shoot it out – at the other end?'

'Yes, yes,' she said impatiently.

'Gosh,' I said again.

But before I could ask any more questions my head suddenly stopped spinning.

And I remembered why we were out here,

'She already knows where we are,' she said. 'I just wanted to get out of that cellar. To fight her on more favourable ground.'

'Fight her?' I gabbled. 'What do you mean, *fight* her? You told me that you've only got the powers of a weedy little cuttlefish. And that she's much more powerful than you.'

'That's right,' Aunt Primrose agreed. 'She is.'

'Then we should run away. Run away now, as fast as we can.'

'We wouldn't get very far,' said Aunt Primrose grimly.

I was petrified. Words came babbling out of my mouth. 'But she'll take me away under the sea and I'll drown and why does she want to take me away . . . ?'

'She likes you,' said Aunt Primrose. 'And

she's lonely – terribly lonely. The loneliness of the Sea Hag is the most terrible loneliness in the world.'

'But I don't want her to like me! Why does she like me? I can't understand it! Why . . . ?'

But I never got the chance to finish my question. Something yanked my feet out from under me.

'It's her!' cried Aunt Primrose. 'She's in the bathing pool!'

'*Aaaargh!*' I yelled, hanging on for dear life to two iron hooks. 'She's pulling me in!'

A tentacle slithered round my ankle. Its suckers were like a hundred tiny grabbing hands.

'*Ugggh!*' I reached down and tore the tentacles away. *Rippp!* It let go of my leg. But another was already snaking round my other leg.

'Help! She's dragging me in!'

I was stretched out like elastic, clinging on to the hooks. I'd have to let go any second. Only my fingertips were holding on and they were slipping, slipping . . .

'LET – HIM – GO!' A voice like

It was like the strange hush before a storm. The seagulls had settled. The bathing pool looked like glass – not a ripple on it. Even the sea had gone quiet. No Aunt Primrose. No Sea Hag. Where had everybody gone?

Then, *fizz*, a few bubbles came up to the top of the bathing pool.

I crept to the edge and looked in.

And there they were – the Sea Hag and Aunt Primrose. In opposite corners like two prize-fighters in a boxing-ring.

It looked like no contest. A white-haired granny in a bathing suit striped like a humbug. Versus the Sea Hag – a pick 'n' mix selection of the most deadly talents of cobra shark, octopus and electric eel.

The Hag's eyes glowed like searchlights. But this time they weren't pointed at me.

They were fixed on Aunt Primrose. Her tentacles writhed about, like they had a life of their own. She'd taken off her Doc Martens. The only bit of her disguise left was her waterproof lipstick. Poppy red lips puffed out from the grey bulgy bag of her head.

I could have saved myself. I could have run away and the Hag wouldn't even have noticed. But I couldn't. Aunt Primrose was in trouble. I couldn't just leave her.

So I crouched down to see what would happen next.

The Hag made the first move. Blast-off!

She shot out an arm like a harpoon. No good. In a blitz of bubbles Aunt Primrose jet-propelled.

'Yay!' I cheered.

But I couldn't see anything. Clouds of sand hid the bottom of the pool.

Then the sand drifted down.

I twitched my specs into place and searched the pool. Where were they? Aunt Primrose was crouched on her chubby legs in one corner. Her eyes were flashing in defiance.

poking up from the sand, was an evil yellow eye. Just one eye, poking up and swivelling.

'A trap! A trap!' I yelled. 'It's an ink trap!'

The purple ink cloud squirted by the Hag dissolved, just sort of fell apart in the water. Aunt Primrose saw it, and knew that she'd been tricked. She froze in her tracks. But it was too late.

Blue light crackled all round her. Her white hair stood on end. Stiff as a kipper, she crashed to the bottom of the pool. The tip of a writhing tentacle began to creep towards her. It was going to wrap itself round her ankle and haul her, ever so slowly, towards that hidden mouth with its seven sets of teeth.

'Aunt Primrose!' I beat at the water desperately. But she couldn't hear.

I started pulling off my shoes, ready to dive in.

Then Aunt Primrose quivered. She flapped like a fish. The tentacles whisked back under the sand. Aunt Primrose came alive.

'Aunt Primrose!' I was nearly crying with joy!

She was still stunned by the Hag's electric shock. She was staggering round in a bubble storm.

Then a grey torpedo shot out of the sand! Shot up to the top of the pool and surfaced right under my nose.

It was the Sea Hag. Aunt Primrose hadn't seen her. But I had. I couldn't miss her. Because she was drifting around on the top of the pool, her tentacles all spread out like party streamers.

Her cobra-shark eyes swivelled round to me. Oh no! But I didn't panic. I whipped off my glasses. But not before I'd seen her wink at me.

'Round three,' she hissed. Then vanished.

I put my specs back on. Just in time to

She did look up. Far, far too late. I saw her mouth – a wide, shocked 'O' shape. Then, *blam*, the Hag dropped right on top of her. And she was squashed by that horrible squirmy body.

'Aunt Primrose!'

I saw a flash of green and gold between the Hag's tentacles. A pink hand got free. It waved pathetically.

Then the Hag shuffled about like a monster chicken on an egg. And the hand went limp.

The fight was over. The Sea Hag had won.

I could already hear that spooky song echoing in my head.

'Under the sea,
Georgie and me, Georgie and me . . .'

Chapter Twelve

Special people are full of surprises. Aunt Primrose had told me that. But I didn't have any surprises up my sleeve. I just slumped on the rocks, feeling hopeless, useless.

'Sorry, Aunt Primrose,' I whispered, trying not to cry.

But somehow, my brain kept on working. It kept pestering me. Asking me questions: 'How do you stop a Sea Hag? How? How?'

'What's the use?' I groaned. 'She's just too powerful.'

But my pesky brain wouldn't give up. 'How? How? How?'

And a tiny idea started to tickle. Then it became a big itch.

'I know how!' I thought, scrambling to

popcorn.

I staggered back through the gate in the wall. My arms were filled with net. It spread out behind me in orange waves.

I fell on my knees by the bathing pool. My heart was beating like bongo drums. But I gave my specs a twitch, then peered into the water.

'Good old Aunt Primrose!'

She'd fought back. Wriggled out from under the Hag. Those whippy tentacles were already reaching for her –

But I was going to use the Sea Hag's tactics. I was going to launch my own surprise attack.

'Geronimo!'

I shoved the net into the pool, then closed my eyes and hoped it was my lucky day. I hadn't aimed it or weighted it or anything. There just wasn't time.

I opened my eyes. The net spread out on the pool's surface. It wasn't going to sink. Yes, it was. It went billowing down, in netty clouds. But who was it going to trap?

I chewed my lips. I couldn't watch. I had to.

There was scuffling down in the pool – a sandstorm, a terrible struggle. Now the sand was clearing –

'Yay!' I jumped up, punched my fist in the air. 'Gotcha. I've gotcha. Ha-ha-ha!'

Aunt Primrose had jet-propelled out of danger. She was hiding behind some ferny seaweed. And the Hag was trapped under folds of heavy net.

It couldn't have worked out better.

I grinned so hard it almost split my face.

The Sea Hag had gone very quiet.

Why wasn't Aunt Primrose climbing out? Why was she still hiding in the weed?

'It's all right,' I called down. 'She can't hurt you now.'

me with her body.

Down in the pool the Hag was swelling like a giant puffer fish. As she swelled her eyes got even madder and colours flashed all over her – bright yellow, purple, shocking pink. She was like a living kaleidoscope! The bathing pool crackled with blue electric fire. The water steamed like a thousand boiling kettles. And all the time, under the net, the Hag was swelling, filling up the pool.

Then, suddenly, the net burst into a million pieces. The Hag exploded out of the pool like a rocket launch, trailing tails of fire. I looked up, but I was blinded, like looking straight into the sun. Aunt Primrose pushed my head down to save my eyes.

We crouched down on the rocks. We

didn't dare look up. Two Sisters Cove grew quiet again. You could hear tiny waves rustling on the rocks.

Then the Sea Hag spoke.

Her voice echoed round the cove. It was as chilly and dark as the deepest sea caves. Just the sound of it made me quiver.

'Did you think you could trap ME in your puny little net? Me? The Sea Hag?'

Very, very slowly, I raised my head.

'Careful,' Aunt Primrose whispered in my ear. 'Don't look into her eyes.'

Too late. I'd already looked. But what I saw was amazing. The Sea Hag was dangling over a rock like a giant octopus. She still had her rosebud lips. But she'd switched off her cobra-shark stare. And in her eyes there was a new expression. What was it? It was hard to tell. But it seemed to be a sort of mixture – of sadness, pain and pride.

I was still trembling like a jelly. 'I don't want to come with you! I don't want to!'

'Don't be afraid, George,' said the Sea Hag in a scornful voice. 'I *promise* I won't try to take you. I'm not interested in you any more. Not in either of you. Nor in

ring like gongs.

'I'm going home!' she cried. She flung a tentacle towards the waves. The sea boiled and foamed as if it were answering her.

'Being ordinary isn't worth it,' said the Sea Hag. 'Afternoon tea just isn't my style! I'm the Sea Hag. I'm going home. I'm going back to the abyss! Alone!'

She began slithering over the rocks. The sea made a terrific din like a mighty orchestra, booming and crashing as if it were welcoming her back.

The Sea Hag's mournful cry was even louder than the sea.

'You know where you are at the bottom of the ocean. You can trust a cobra shark. You can trust a cobra shark more than you can trust people!'

I thought she was going. But, suddenly, she turned to me again. She seemed to have completely forgotten her promise!

'This is your last chance, George,' she coaxed in her silkiest voice. 'Won't you come with me?' She swept her tentacle round the bay. 'Do you know how much of this planet is ocean, George? Nearly three-quarters of it! It's so cramped in your little land-world, George. Come to *my* world. Come and explore it. Come and roam the seven seas with me!'

Aunt Primrose gripped my arm. 'Don't listen to her,' she said urgently. 'Don't look into her eyes. Take your specs off!'

But this time, I didn't need to take my specs off. I just shook my head at the Sea Hag. 'I can't come with you,' I told her. 'You know I can't. I'll drown.'

The Sea Hag turned her great eyes on Aunt Primrose.

'So he doesn't know yet?' she said in surprise.

Aunt Primrose gave a tiny shake of the head.

'I'm not coming!' I said again.

'Fool,' hissed the Hag. But she didn't

Then nothing.

'Violet!' called Aunt Primrose.

But there was only a little crowd of bubbles where the Sea Hag had been. Then, one by one, they popped.

'She's gone,' said Aunt Primrose.

There was a strange stinging feeling in my eyes. And I was really surprised to hear myself murmuring, 'Poor Sea Hag. Poor, lonely Sea Hag.'

'Will she ever come back?' I asked Aunt Primrose.

She put her arm round my shoulders and gave me a hug. We started walking back towards the house.

'No,' Aunt Primrose said. 'I don't think she ever will. I think she's given up on the human race. She's gone back to the fishes.'

'What did she mean,' I asked Aunt

Primrose, 'when she sort of stared at you and said, "So he doesn't know yet?" What don't I know?'

'Ahh . . .' said Aunt Primrose. She took a deep breath, as if she was going to start a long explanation.

But she didn't get the chance.

For just at that moment, far, far out at sea, a shooting star climbed out of dark blue water.

'It's her!' I cried.

In a burst of glittering light the Sea Hag curved across the sky. Then she plunged back into the sea. She left behind a wonderful golden rainbow.

It was her final farewell.

'Beautiful,' I said. 'She's really beautiful, isn't she?'

'She certainly is,' said Aunt Primrose. 'Beautiful – but deadly, unfortunately. You can't trust her an inch.'

She waved her hand in a last salute. 'Goodbye, Violet,' she called out. 'Goodbye, my dear sister.'

And slowly, very slowly, the rainbow faded away.

'I can't believe it,' Mum said, frowning at her diary. 'These school holidays really do creep up on one. It doesn't seem two minutes since your last one.'

I looked up from my book, *The Amazing World of Fish*. It was a present from Aunt Primrose for my eleventh birthday. It had arrived this morning. Right on time.

'So, birthday boy,' said Mum, 'what's it to be this summer? Your dad and I can manage a week at the end of August. Almost certainly. But that leaves,' she flicked over the pages, 'five weeks to fill in.'

She waved a glossy brochure at me. 'Now what about an Activity Holiday? Just look at these children. They look as if they're having lots of fun, don't they?'

I sighed and closed Aunt Primrose's book. I said to Mum, 'Did you know there are ice fish that live in the Antarctic and have anti-freeze in their blood? So they don't freeze solid like ice-pops?'

'Very nice, dear,' she said. But she looked a bit startled. Just like she did when we were going round the supermarket and I filled the trolley with crabsticks.

She said, 'What on earth do you want those for?'

And I said, 'You should try one. They're really tasty!'

I nibbled a crabstick as I looked at the brochure she gave me. There were two children, in yellow climbing helmets, being lowered down a cliff.

'They look scared stiff to me,' I told Mum.

'No, they don't!' she said. 'They're having a lovely time! Now don't be difficult, George; you know the summer holidays are a real headache. Look, I could book you in here for a few weeks. Pony-trekking in Wales! Wouldn't that be great?'

'Or,' I said, 'I could go to Aunt Prim-

you stand it? For the whole summer holidays. Isn't it a teeny-weeny bit boring with
Aunt Primrose?'

'I think I can stand it,' I said.

'We'll buy you a present,' said Dad, busy
at his computer screen.

'You're already buying me a present,'
I reminded him. 'It's my birthday today,
remember? We're going to choose some
fish this afternoon.'

Mum and Dad threw worried looks at
each other. Dad shut down his computer.
He swivelled his chair round.

'We've been meaning to ask you about
that, George,' he said. 'Are you sure you
want real live fish? In a tank? I mean,
they're not exactly hi-tech, are they?
Wouldn't you rather have fish on a floppy
disc? There are some very exciting biology

packages out on CD Rom. The fish look as if they're really alive!'

'I want fish that *are* really alive,' I said.

Dad shrugged. 'Well, it's your present.'

I opened my book again and took a bite from my crabstick.'

'Did you know,' I told Dad, 'that there are fish called mud skippers that walk out of the water and climb trees?'

Mum and Dad tiptoed out of the room. But I could hear them whispering in puzzled voices behind the door.

'I suppose,' whispered Mum, 'it's because he's eleven now. I mean, there are bound to be *changes* at eleven, aren't there?'

Two hours later Dad and I were standing in the fish section of Pet World. I was looking at some goldfish.

Dad was grilling the sales assistant. 'So what exactly do I get for my money if I take your advice and buy this more expensive water pump?'

I stopped listening to them. I was in a world of my own. An orange fish, with a big head like a bulldog, blew bubbles at

believe it. I twitched my specs up my nose
and looked again.

No mistake.

My hand looked like a block of Neapolitan ice-cream! It was striped in layers of
strawberry, vanilla, chocolate, just like the
fish I was waving at.

The fish in the tank was getting very
excited. It darted about in a swirl of
bubbles. It bumped the glass as if it was
trying to get out.

I closed my eyes and wished, very hard,
that my mind was playing tricks. I opened
my eyes. The colours were spreading, like
some awful creeping infection! They were
on both hands now. I shoved my hands
deep into my coat pockets. I looked around
– nobody was watching. So I started

whistling casually, as if nothing had happened.

Then I caught sight of my reflection in the glass side of the tank.

'I don't believe this! I'm a freak! I'm an alien!'

Climbing up my neck, from under my T-shirt, was a wavy line of chocolate brown. Followed by white. Followed by –

'*Aaaargh!*' I zipped my coat right up. I put my hood up and pulled the drawstring tight so that there was only a tiny little hole to see out of.

I rushed up to Dad and grabbed his arm. 'Come on, Dad, come on! We've got to go!'

Dad looked down. 'I can't go now, George. I'm doing some research on this fish thing. Getting a few facts and figures.'

'Never mind that!' I gabbled at him through the hole in the hood. I rushed for the door.

Dad strode after me into the car park.

'Look, George,' he said. 'I'm trying to be reasonable here. Doing my best to understand. But what's going on? I thought

handle. 'Open this car. I've got to get home. I've got to make an urgent phone call to Aunt Primrose.'

The car slid out of the car park of Pet World. I could see Dad staring at me in the driving mirror. He put on some classical music to calm himself down.

At home I raced up to the bathroom, locked the door and tore off my coat.

'Phew! Thank goodness!'

I breathed a big sigh of relief. The Neapolitan ice-cream stripes had gone. I checked in the bathroom mirror. I wasn't a freak. Or an alien. I was back to normal.

I touched my neck, where the stripes had been, just to make sure.

Then I snatched my hand back as if it were red hot.

My hand crept up to my neck again.

I turned sideways, looked in the mirror and lifted up the hair behind my ears . . .

Then I went racing downstairs again.

'Mum! Mum!'

Mum wasn't in the kitchen. But Dad was. He was opening and shutting doors, looking for something.

I tugged at his shirt. 'Dad, Dad, what happened when you were eleven? Did anything weird happen to you? Did you get webbed toes, or fins or anything? Did you get slime glands?'

'Do you know where Mrs Perkins keeps the coffee?' asked Dad, with his head stuck in a cupboard.

I rushed into the living-room.

Mum was on the telephone. 'Shhhhh,' she warned. 'This is work.'

I jiggled about. I couldn't help myself. I had to grab my right hand to stop it feeling about behind my ear.

At last, Mum put down the phone.

'I've got lumps behind my ear!' I yelled at her. 'Behind both my ears!'

'All right, George. No need to deafen me. Just calm down.'

Mum felt my neck. '*Hmmm,*' she said.

Harumph! Yes, I think I have.'

I felt weak with relief. I'd just got a cold, that was all. Just an ordinary boring old cold. Everybody gets *them*.

'Well, I hope you don't have to stay off school,' said Mum. 'It would be very inconvenient right now. You're not faking it, are you?'

'Of course I'm not! How can I fake lumps?'

'Well, I've got to admit you're a very peculiar colour,' said Mum. 'Do you feel ill or anything? Could it be all those crabsticks you've been eating?'

'What colour?' I gasped in a sort of strangled voice. 'What colour am I?'

I tried very hard to feel ill. But I didn't feel ill at all. I felt horribly healthy.

'You're a sort of green,' said Mum.

'Lime green in fact. And wait a minute, you're a sort of yellow as well. Bright yellow! It's quite spectacular! I've never seen anything like it!'

'I've got to make a phone call,' I said, weakly. 'A private one, in the study.'

And I staggered on bendy legs through the study door.

W ith trembling fingers I punched in Aunt Primrose's number.

The phone rang and rang.

'Please be there,' I wished. 'Please be there.'

Then she picked up the phone. 'Hello?'

Her voice was as clear as the bathing pool. She could have been standing right next to me.

'Aunt Primrose, Aunt Primrose, I've got to talk to you. Strange things are happening to me. Uncontrollable things. I've got this book called *Growing Up*. It says about getting hairy and getting a deeper voice. But it doesn't say anything about green and yellow stripes and –'

'Ah, George,' interrupted Aunt

Primrose calmly. 'Happy eleventh birth-day, George. I was expecting you to call.'

'I'm a freak!' I gabbled into the phone. 'I keep changing colour!'

'Congratulations,' said Aunt Primrose in the same calm voice. 'And you are defin-itely NOT a freak. You are special. I told you that.'

'But I don't want to be special! I don't want to be different at all! People that are different get picked on. I mean, what will they think at school? You even get picked on for wearing specs. What's it going to be like if I get slime glands or something? They'll think I'm an alien from the planet Zarg!'

'For heaven's sake,' said Aunt Primrose. 'You must get things in perspective. We all have our little differences. Some people have belly-buttons that go in. Some people have belly-buttons that stick out. But they're not freaks, are they?'

'I'm not talking about belly-buttons!' I roared down the phone. 'I'm talking about –' Then a truly terrible thought burst into my brain. 'I won't turn into a

What will I get then.

'Oh,' said Aunt Primrose, 'just the usual things that run in the family. Nothing out of the ordinary. The changing colour thing. And perhaps gills, if you're lucky. Have you got any suspicious lumps?'

'Yes,' I said. 'But they're swollen glands. Mum said so.'

'I wouldn't bet on it,' said Aunt Primrose.

'But I've got a cold!' I coughed down the phone. '*Harumph! Harumph!*'

'We'll see,' said Aunt Primrose.

'But I'll be a freak! How can I be anything else? With gills and wavy lines all over me like a telly that's gone wrong. People will point at me in the street. They'll laugh at me. They'll say, "There goes George, that Fishy Freak!"'

'No, they won't,' insisted Aunt Primrose. 'They won't even notice. The colour changes are a bit alarming at first. But you can control them. I'll teach you how. And no one need see your gills. Just keep your hair long, that's all. And another tip. Don't practise jet propulsion in the bath. You can have a very nasty accident that way.'

'Jet propulsion? Will I be able to do that?'

'You might.'

'Wow!' I said. I couldn't help thinking how impressed my friends would be, when I jet-propelled in the swimming pool.

'And you might even get bio-luminescence,' added Aunt Primrose cheerily.

'What's that?' I asked suspiciously.

'Lots of deep-sea fishes have it. It means that bits of your body glow in the dark.'

'Which bits?'

'Well, I'm not sure. You'll have to wait to find out. That way, it'll be a big surprise, won't it?'

'Yes,' I said, in a stunned voice. 'A very big surprise . . .'

'I'm coming in two weeks,' I told her. 'I can stay for nearly all summer.'

'Perfect,' said Aunt Primrose. 'We've got a lot of talking to do.'

'Shall I tell Mum and Dad?' I asked her. 'You know, about being special?'

'I wouldn't bother,' said Aunt Primrose. 'They'll only think it's inconvenient.'

'OK,' I said, relieved.

'And whatever you do, don't worry! It's not so bad, having cuttlefish skills. It's very good fun actually.'

'Another thing,' I said. 'Another thing I want to ask you. Why isn't Dad a cuttlefish?'

'Oh, he's just unlucky,' said Aunt Primrose. 'He didn't inherit the family talents. They skip some people. Don't

know why. He's an accountant, isn't he?'
  'Yes.'
  'Ah, well,' said Aunt Primrose mysteriously. 'That probably explains it then.'

Aunt Primrose and I were taking an early morning stroll round Two Sisters Cove.

I'd been there for two days. And in that time I'd done nothing but ask questions, questions and more questions.

I asked her another one. 'What happened to the Sea Hag's precious?'

Aunt Primrose knew exactly what I meant.

'Oh, I let her octopus go,' she said. 'I let everything in the cellar go – the puffer fish and the electric eel and the cobra shark. She only kept them for company – for someone to talk to. And for when she got peckish, of course.'

I shivered. Sometimes I felt really sorry

for the Sea Hag. And other times, I knew that what Aunt Primrose said was true. You couldn't trust her an inch.

I said, for about the millionth time, 'I'm glad I won't become a Sea Hag.'

'You might not even become a cuttle-fish,' said Aunt Primrose. 'Those lumps behind your ear don't seem to be doing much. Perhaps your mum was right. Perhaps they are just swollen glands after all.'

I felt one of the lumps. I was sure I could feel four little ridges. I would be sorry if they didn't turn into gills. I'd got used to the idea of being different. I was even look-ing forward to it. I couldn't wait to see my friends' faces when I jet-propelled in swimming lessons. Or when bits of my body glowed in the dark.

'Will I get slime glands?' I asked Aunt Primrose hopefully.

She had told me that some eels have slime glands. And they can fill a bucket with green slime in two minutes!

But Aunt Primrose shook her head. 'Very, very unlikely,' she said.

'At least I can do the colour changes,' I
said proudly.

jumping purple
spots.

'Bravo!' smiled Aunt Primrose. 'You've
been practising. Soon I'll teach you how
to talk to fishes. But don't go chatting to
any cobra sharks.'

'No way!' I said. 'Not unless I take my
specs off first.'

We walked a bit further along the beach.

Then I said, 'I've got another question,
I'm afraid.'

'Fire away,' said Aunt Primrose.

'Do you remember when I was little you
came to our house?'

'Yes, I remember.'

'And you asked me a riddle – *The more
you take, the more you leave behind*?'

'Yes.'

'Well, what's the answer to that riddle?'

'Look behind you, George,' she said.

I turned round. All I could see was a wide empty beach with two lines of footprints on it. I was puzzled for a minute.

Then I gave a big grin. I said, 'I know! I know the answer! The answer is footprints, isn't it? Footprints in the sand.'

'That's right,' said Aunt Primrose.

'That's easy-peasy!' I said. 'Why didn't I guess that before? It was so simple. And I was trying to make it difficult.'

'Some things are like that,' said Aunt Primrose. 'You worry away, making things difficult, making them ever so complicated. When really, it's all very simple.'

I knew what she was talking about. 'You mean, like colour-changing? Like having gills and stuff?'

'That's right,' she said. 'There's nothing to it.'

'Nothing to it at all,' I agreed.

And we walked back to the house, talking all the way. While around us the sun turned Two Sisters Cove to gold.